NEW POEMS BOOK FOUR

NEW POEMS BOOK FOUR

Charles Bukowski

Edited by John Martin

Ben —
Here's a
rational for being
drinking and that.
crazy — not that we need
one —
Dad

These poems are part of an archive of unpublished work that Charles Bukowski left to be published after his death.

Grateful acknowledgement is made to John Martin, who edited these poems.

This edition first published in 2005 by
Virgin Books Ltd
Thames Wharf Studios
Rainville Road
London
W6 9HA

First published in the United States of America in 2005 by Ecco, as *Slouching Toward Nirvana*

Published in arrangement with Ecco, an imprint of HarperCollins Publishers, Inc., New York, New York USA

A catalogue record for this book is available from the British Library.

ISBN 0 7535 1036 7

Typeset by Phoenix Photosetting, Chatham, Kent
Printed and bound in Great Britain by Mackays of Chatham, Kent

CONTENTS

PART ONE

Bach is the hardest to play badly because
he made so few spiritual mistakes.

A 4TH OF JULY IN THE EARLY 30'S

there wasn't much to celebrate,
of course,
our fathers weren't working
and the canned food from the Dept. of Relief
all had the same terrible
stale taste.
nothing much was happening anywhere and
there was a joyless resignation
in the air
but I remember this one morning at about
6 a.m. on the 4th of July
1932 or 3 or 4, I don't remember which,
when I heard loud explosions
in the street outside:
GIANT FIRECRACKERS!

I got out of bed, dressed
quickly, ran outside
and there
coming up Longwood Avenue
right in the center of the street was
my buddy Gene
walking along and throwing
giant firecrackers
into the air.

the morning fog
was just beginning to lift
and the first sun was coming
through
and there was Gene
walking
along

and making the air
explode!

I ran up to him.
"god damn! what you got?"

"cherry bombs!
and plenty of
them!"

he also had
what was called a "punk,"
a coated metal stick that
glowed hot and red at the
end.

Gene touched the punk
to a fuse
watched it burn down,
then tossed the bomb high
into the air
where it exploded
right at the height of its
arc.

a man came out
on his front porch
in his pajamas.

"HEY, YOU KIDS, CUT OUT THAT
SHIT! I WANT TO SLEEP!"
"come out here and make us
stop!" said Gene
(he was big for his
age).

"I'LL TELL YOUR FATHER!"

Gene laughed, lit a cracker,
and tossed it toward the
man. it landed
right on the ledge of his large
plate glass window.

"BAANNGG!!"

luckily the window didn't
break.

the man ran back into his
house.

Gene handed me the punk
and a bomb.

"you try one . . ."

I lit the fuse and waited
as long as I dared
then hurled the bomb.
it went off a dozen feet over my
head.

"not bad," Gene said.

we walked up Longwood to
21st street, took a left, then
went up the little hill.

"watch this,"
said Gene.

there was a garbage can sitting out by a
fence.
Gene took the lid off, dropped
a lit bomb in there and
put the lid back
on.

"BAANNNGG!!"

the explosion sent the lid flying
about 3 feet
into the air.

"god, they're powerful!"

"yeah," said Gene.

we walked a little further up
the hill.
there was a car parked there
with the window slightly open
on the driver's
side.

"watch this," said Gene.

he lit a cracker and dropped it
through the window.

"BAAANNNGG!!"

the car rocked, then
was filled with thick
blue smoke.

"that was great!" I
said.

Gene had 3 or 4 cherry bombs left.
we turned, walked back down
the hill.

Gene lit the last ones,
one by one and arched them
as far as possible
into the air where
they exploded.

then we were standing in front of
his house.
it was now about 6:30
a.m.

"well, that's it," he said,
"it's over."

"thanks, Gene."

"sure, see you
around . . ."

he walked into his
house.

I walked to mine,
opened the front door,
entered, walked down
the hall.

my father heard me from
his bedroom.

"where the hell you
been?"

"out celebrating . . ."

"good for you, son!
it's a great country
we live in!"

I walked back to my bedroom,
undressed, got back
into bed.

he's got it all wrong as usual,
I thought,
I was only celebrating
myself.

WITHOUT STRESS OR AGONY

they sit down
get comfortable
talk and
complain and
wave their arms
they have nothing else to
do
and since they have
nothing else to do
they'd prefer to do it
in your company.

I am astonished at the
number of people with
nothing to do
but get comfortable
talk
complain and
wave their arms.

tirelessly
they knock on many doors
looking for other
people with
nothing to do

and when they talk
or complain
their speech is
without stress or agony
they're more like a mild nervous
affliction with
nowhere to go.

sometimes I simply ask them
to leave
and they do
and then I feel guilty
as if I had perhaps misunderstood
their need
or I feel that I may have offended
them.

not so.
they return
they always return
each and every one of them
they sit down again
get comfortable
talk
complain and
wave their arms.

but I know
that I am not the only one
who suffers thus.

they go from one to another
from here to there
and while they are with another
I get the one who has just been
elsewhere
and then
a new visitor sits down
gets comfortable
talks
complains and
waves their arms
at me.

MY CLOSE CALL

not a good fighter, he managed to get into some brutal
back-alley fights.

because of his darkened mind and too much to drink, he always
picked the biggest meanest fucker he could find.
winging and catching shots to the shouts of the
whore bystanders, he took some lovely beatings some
of the time.

"Hank," his best friend told him one night, "we want you to join
the gang."

"I can't."

"can't? why?"

"I got something else to do . . ."

2 days later one of the gang was wounded in a police
shoot-out and 2 others killed,
including his friend.

he went to a bar 3 blocks east, sat waiting for
an answer, sat waiting for
the moon to change into the sun,
sat waiting patiently for one thing
or another.

CLOTHES COST MONEY

Hofstetter wore knickers with
kneesocks, the only kid in school
who dressed like that, only he didn't
dress himself, his mother dressed
him and to top it off he wore
large horn-rimmed glasses and he had
a very fat white face, in fact his
whole body was soft and white and fat,
and he wore bright checkered sweaters,
a different color
sweater each day, and he had the
strangest shoes—large, square, clumsy
orthopedic shoes, black,
and it was a long walk from grammar
school to where Hofstetter lived,
maybe 12 blocks, and I walked home
with him each day after school
but he never made it safely home,
the gang followed him each day,
taunting, calling him names, throwing
rocks, spitting on him until they
finally closed in to give him his
daily treat.

they were older and
there were 5 or 6 of them and they
thrashed him well, chops to the
neck, fists to the face, and down
he'd go, again and again, silently,
taking his beating almost as a ritual,
rising to be smashed down again,
his bloody nose dripping onto
his brightly colored sweater,

his face glistening with tears, the
late afternoon sun reflecting on
them, and the knees of his knickers
now torn and dirtied, the
flesh showing through as he was
knocked down again and again
until he no longer rose and
then they slowly left, that gang of
5 or 6, still shouting vile
threats.

it happened day after day
after day.

I always helped him up then
gathering his books and his notebook
from where they'd been tossed
with the papers torn loose and
I helped him walk back home
his stockings dragging, his glasses
half on often with one lens
gone.

as he entered his house
day after day after day
I sat on the lawn in front and
listened while his mother
screamed, "YOU'VE
RUINED YOUR CLOTHES AGAIN!
DON'T YOU KNOW THAT CLOTHES
COST MONEY?"

Hofstetter never replied,
and then I would hear his mother
slap him and he would scream
as
his mother kept slapping

him, "YOU'VE RUINED YOUR CLOTHES
AGAIN!
DON'T YOU KNOW THAT CLOTHES
COST MONEY?"

I would leave then.

the next day I would see
Hofstetter again at school, again
dressed in knickers, his brightly
colored checkered sweaters, his
square, clumsy, black orthopedic
shoes and they would begin on him
early—putting gum on his seat,
dropping itching powder down the
back of his neck, zapping him with
spit-wads with their home-
made slingshots while the
teacher was absorbed with the
lesson . . .
the hot Los Angeles
sun came through the windows,
the blackboards were
formal, dull and uninspiring
as Hofstetter sat there
waiting for the last bell
and the walk home, day after
day after day, it never
changed, it couldn't and
would never change,
that horrible march home,
that little-known history of
inhumanity.

AN EASY WAY TO DIE

is talking about writing while signing
your published tomes in a
bookstore as cars swish by outside in the rain
and authors living and dead sit all around
you on their shelves.
you suck on a green bottle of beer
while the people sit and watch you sign your books.
something inside you keeps saying,
what the hell am I doing?
this isn't me sitting here signing books,
this is some fat old fool relaxing in the shade of nowhere.
I should get up and crack one of these
suckers over the head with this bottle,
I should scream,
"I WON'T DO THIS SHIT!"
but look at me:
nice old guy, smiling, talking about Faulkner,
talking about the racetrack,
talking about . . . what?

this is the ultimate sellout, Jack.
you are letting them cover you with salve
and cream.
did you fight your way off the park bench
just to do this?

finally, you shove the books aside,
"I've got to go."

"that's all right, that's all right, thank
you very much."

you get up, shake hands.
you are the author, hey, hey, you're
not really crazy after all, are you?

they've tamed your ass.

"thanks very much," they say
again.

"sure, sure," you answer, then you're
out the door
into the night
carrying what bits are left of you
in your pocket, in your shoe, in
your graying hair.

and not very much is left:
they took away the tiger and left a
pussycat
as you meow yourself to your car and
get the fuck out of
there.

WE HAVE HAND GUNS AROUND HERE

they broke in and stole
the old Jewish lady's
red Irish setter.
it's nearly all she had except
for her New York accent.

then they came back
and stole her hair dryer
and 4 large cans of Starkist
chunk-style tuna.

her son has come by
with a dozen cardboard cartons
he found behind the
supermarket.

he's moving her,
he says, to a safer
part of town.

now, I thought, where can
that be?

I ought to ask him while
she stands there waiting
in the center of the
lawn but I think he's in a
hurry.

MAKING DO

once
on this ball-busting
job
I asked the worker
next to
me,
"how do we know
we haven't died
and gone to
hell?"

he didn't
reply.
he
thought I was
crazy to imagine
we might have
gone to
hell.

the fact
was:
he was not
in
hell, I
was.

I
looked at the
other
workers.
they didn't think
they were
in hell
either.

the foreman
walked up
behind
me.

"Chinaski,
what are you
looking around
for?"

"I
want to see
where I
am."

"you're here at the
A-Gleam Lighting
Company."

"thanks."

"and no talking

on the
job."

"what?"

"I saw you
talking to
Meyers."

"o.k."

"stay on top
of your job,
Chinaski."

he walked
off.

"Meyers," I
said, "I think
I'm in
hell!"

he still didn't
reply.

I
looked at
the wall
clock:
25 minutes
until lunch,
30 minutes
for lunch,
then
5 more
hours
plus 2 hours

overtime,
an hour to
drive home,
ten minutes
to
bathe,
30 minutes to
eat,
20 minutes
to read the
paper
and in
another
hour
you'd be
asleep,
only
to wake
up in the
morning,
dress,
get a quick
coffee,
then
an
hour to
drive
back in
plus
half-a-day
on Saturday
and then
back on
Monday.

then I
heard Meyers
hissing:

"you
son-of-a-bitch, if
you don't
like the
job,
quit!"

"Meyers, I'm
proud of
you, you
spoke to
me!"

then the
foreman was
behind me
again.

"Chinaski,
what did
I tell
you
about
talking?"

"you
told me
not
to."

"well?"

"but
now you're

making me
talk!"

"don't be
a wise
guy."

he walked
off.

"Jesus, Meyers,
I almost got
canned!"

the little bastard
didn't
even look at
me.

"and Meyers,
the next time
you call me a
son-of-a-
bitch,
I'm going to
knock you
on your
ass!"

now it
was his
turn
to watch
the clock and
wonder.

RARE INDEED

a man sent me an autograph from
Beau Jack.
he said that Beau Jack asked him
to send it on to
me.
I told the man to tell
Beau Jack that I was
honored.
have you heard of
him?
he was a prizefighter.
many men box but he was a
fighter, a terror,
a champion.
Beau Jack.
the chills still
run up and down my
spine.
you just can't
know how good it
feels to
hear
from
him.

THE POET

many of his poems refer to THE POET,
he sometimes alludes to the streets or to the moon but
most often
he speaks of THE POET—poem after poem is about
THE POET
until you hope never to hear of THE POET again.

this poetic descendant of the 17th century
with the Brooklyn accent
hasn't had much luck (lately)
which makes him all the more certain of his immortality:
popularity is a sign of spiritual decay:
how can a man (me) who
once puked up his guts in unpaid rented rooms
but who now owns his own home and drives a
BMW
remain a fucking genius?

this POET, when we were both on the skids,
dressed worse than I, his shirt always stained
with drink, with
buttons missing and his big gut punching through,
the zipper on his pants at half-mast, but THIS POET
always wore a bright clean scarf at the throat
(this indicated the POET part) and between drinking
my booze and snoring away the nights on my broken-
down couch
he managed to continually
proclaim himself a POET
in a very LOUD voice as if the gods were listening.
perhaps they were, I surely was.

"Jesus," I'd tell him, "let up a bit."

but THE POET talked on and on.

I haven't seen him in some years
but people keep me informed
about him:

"he's on SSI."

"he's in Denver."

"he went back to New York."

life goes on but the POETS
never stop: the good and the bad continue.
sometimes I receive unsolicited lit mags in the mail
and there *he* will be, still writing
poems about THE POET, or sometimes writing
essays about THE POET, and I read these with some
interest because he often mentions me
and other poet ex-friends
insisting that we all are finished as
writers,
he can't seem to let go of that notion, which doesn't make
sense to me: I mean when you bury a man, just leave
a rose and walk away.

I thumb through those lit mags,
and sometimes there are pictures, he's most often
photographed with other old Beats, those kittens
still hanging together, wondering where the good times
went, looking sad and confused as the young girls jump
into bed with a new generation; the
old Beats look fat, haggard and angry like ancient
prostitutes still flashing their faded garter belts;
they pose for the camera like
long-retired door-to-door salesmen
photographed together at some ill-advised
reunion.

my POET, his gut is bigger than ever,
his hair has gone white—that's no sin—but I don't
understand his unrealistic rage at the
corner he's backed into; but then
I take that back: he was surely more
clever than I: I always worked for others, for corporations
and
sweatshops, I tossed away minutes, hours, years doing
the
most menial tasks, going in day after day, night after
night with my ass dragging on the floor
—while *he* survived solely by being THE
POET, perhaps not in the grandest manner, but he
was never nailed down to an 8-hour job, he was always
just
THE POET, and now, since I'm clearly finished as a writer
and
too fucking old for the 8-hour job, I'll just be
forced to cruise about in my BMW and wait for the arrival
of that last, precious sunset.

BOLERO

listening to Ravel now, the *Bolero*,
I'm thinking about when I was a
kid, there was a movie
and George Raft was in it and he was
a dancer and it was near the end of
the movie and he had been shot,
shot bad, a bullet or maybe more,
and he was hurt but determined to finish
his dance to the tune of Ravel's
Bolero and he went on and on

dancing and you could see that
his wounds were getting to him
but he narrowed his eyes and
danced to the end and I mean,
I was impressed.
I wanna be like George Raft, I
thought.

now maybe
a decade or something passes
and I am at the Del Mar racetrack,
I'm a drunk and a gambler, have
women troubles
and it's after the 2nd race,
and I've walked around and now I want
to lay a bet
but I can't get up the stairway,
there's a crowd in the way
and I try to push through
and I ask somebody, "what the hell's
the matter here? did somebody die?"
"no," he answered, "it's George Raft!"
"god damn it!" I say,
"I want to place my bet!"
I push through the crowd
and sure enough, halfway up the
stairway,
there stands George Raft,
he has on his soft hat
pulled down low over one eye
he looks as tough as ever
and he is slouched against the
rail, more or less
posing,
the crowd gawking.

"GOD DAMN IT!" I yell, "LET ME
THROUGH!"

"it's George Raft," somebody tells
me.

I push through then and as
I pass Raft I say,
"I DON'T GIVE A DAMN IF YOU ARE
GEORGE RAFT, I WANT TO BET!"

he just looks at me and doesn't
say anything.

I go to the window and lay down my
bet.
it's 3 minutes to post.
I walk to the bar and order
a scotch and water.
I have a hangover and a two-day
beard.

I slam my drink down and
go out to watch them
run.

what happens is that you watch a
movie and then—bang!—you become the
movie.

now the horses spring out of the gate
and the *Bolero* is playing just for me!
the beautiful girls dance and
smile
as the world spins in the sun
as my jock comes racing past
his silks flashing before my eyes
and as he rides my horse

like a blazing bat out of
hell, I cry, "come on! come on,
you son-of-a-bitch!"

A WINTER MEMORY

job #15 was in Philadelphia, a parts warehouse on
Fairmount near
16th., 65 cents an hour, right after World War II at SNAP-
OFF-TOOLS.
the manager was a bright good-looking boy, fine posture,
raven hair, movie star looks, just out of the navy. his
favorite saying
was, "we do the impossible first and the rest later on!" I
asked to
speak to him one day and said, "look, 65 cents an hour
isn't very
much, how about a dime more?" he explained that things
were very
tight, it was impossible, they couldn't do it, and besides,
"Tommy is
only getting 55 cents an hour." Tommy was a 16-year-old
albino
with three fingers missing on his right hand.

I had to take the packages to the post office each
afternoon in a
wooden pushcart with 2 big wheels. I'd done that kind of
work
before with bolts of cloth in New York City. SNAP-OFF-
TOOLS
was next to a bar I frequented each night and although I
tried to
sneak my cart past the bar entrance somebody in there

would always
see me, usually one of the hookers. "well, Big Time,
where ya' goin'
with the rickshaw? ha, ha, ha!"

I came in hung over most mornings and silently and
efficiently did
my work. nobody bothered me until at the end of two
weeks Tommy
walked up and said, "aren't you happy?" I said, "happy?
why?" he
said, "*I'm* happy." "good," I said, "go away." then he said,
"you ought
to be happy because today is *payday*!" "but Tommy, we've
worked for
two weeks!" "I know," he said, "but you see today we get
it all at
once!"

the middle of the next week I phoned in sick. I was sitting
in the bar
that morning about 10:30 when Tommy came in to buy
a pack of
cigarettes for the manager. Tommy saw me at the bar.
Marie, the
hooker, was telling me her troubles and buying me draft
beers.
I got to Tommy before he reached the door. "look, kid,
there's no
need to tell anybody that you saw me in here." "oh no,"
he said, "I
won't tell anybody."

the next morning they let me work ten minutes, then the
manager
called me into the front office. "you phoned in sick

yesterday and

then you were seen in the bar next door," he said. "who saw me?" "it

doesn't matter," he said, "what matters is that you lied to us." "no lie,"

I said, "I was very sick." "what were you doing in the bar?" "when a

man is sick a bar is the best place to be," I replied. "we're letting you

go. you have 3 days' pay coming." he handed me a little yellow

envelope. they paid in cash.

in the bar I opened the yellow envelope: there were two fives, three

ones, three quarters and three pennies.

"shit!" said Marie, "you're *rich*! I'll have a whiskey with a soda back!"

"give me 2 Buds in the bottle!" said Lilly the Dopester. "gimme a

draft beer!" said Frogman. "give me a glass of water and some

change," I said.

about an hour later Tommy walked in for a pack of cigarettes. 16 is

pretty young to be buying smokes in a bar. he saw me in the mirror. I

got to Tommy before he reached the door. I held him by the arm and

looked at him. "I didn't tell anybody," he said, "honest, I didn't tell

anybody!" I let go of his arm and he ran out.

when I sat back down Marie said, "molesting young boys now?"

I told her that yes I was and would she like to drive to Camden that
night with me to catch the fights?

LIVING IN A GREAT BIG WAY

nothing ever happened in the Mexican bar, I went
night after night but nobody ever threatened me and I
got tired of that and found an illegal Chinese bar hidden
behind a deserted warehouse and I drank away the nights
there
trying to forget that I was a stock boy at the May Company
department store and
after the bar closed I'd go back to my room and stretch
out in the dark.

each day when I arrived at the May Company I'd put on my
brown smock and take supplies to the various departments,
rolling along with my green cart, I was always
hung over but nobody ever noticed and the other stock
boys never spoke to me.

it was always the same, the Chinese bar at night and my green
cart during the day.

I had the feeling that I could break anybody in half,
just pick them up and snap them in two but I was
always polite, excessively so.

then it happened, I got into a fist fight in a
storage room with a stock boy called Bobby and he
beat the hell out of me.

then that night I got into a fight with a Chinaman and
he beat the hell out of me too.

so I took the bus to Houston, got a job in a gas station
and switched from wine to vodka.

THEN AND NOW

let's call him Harry Keel.
he was in my life for some
time—from grammar school
up through junior
high.
he bloodied many a
boy against that wire
fence
at school,
trapping him there
as we
watched.
I wasn't one of those
boys, I wasn't considered
a challenge.

Harry Keel could hit a
baseball farther, he could
run
faster
than any of us.
he had a way of walking,
he had a way of
talking,
he had a way of
doing things.

we all admired and feared
Harry Keel.

in Jr. High, he was the
first to shave,
he had a coarse black
beard.
also, he wore his
shirt
open
and you could see
the curling black
hair on his
chest.

and damn,
he was good at
basketball,
football,
handball,
the high jump,
the long jump,
the pole vault,
the shot put
and
gymnastics.

we wondered as
we watched him
talking to the girls
in the hall
or out on the front
lawn
or in some secluded
corner.

he was the first to
get an
automobile
and,
I'm sure,
the first to get
laid.

all of us wanted to
be like
Harry Keel.

when he graduated
he went on to a
different high
school than I
did.

two decades went by
before I saw Harry
Keel again.

I was working in a
light fixture plant as a
packer.

I looked up
and there he was
dressed in a wrinkled
suit with a dirty shirt
and a loose
necktie.
his shoes were
scuffed.

he was now a salesman.
and he was trying to

sell something
to the owner
of the shop.

from the look on Harry's
face
he wasn't having much
luck.

and strangely,
Harry Keel had
shrunk.
there was fear in his
eyes,
his neck had grown
thin
and his head
hung
down.

but I knew it was
Harry.
I knew him well from all those
early years.

so, there he was.

even now
chances were
he made more money
than I did.

but there I was
barrel-chested
in my white
T-shirt,
muscles hardened from
years of

hard labor
ten hours a
day.
I was the mean and
crazy white
guy,
full of humor, laughter
and gamble.
I was shacked with a
silken-legged
beauty.
I drank and fought all
night,
was the terror of the
local bars
and the best damned
packer in the shop,
loved by the Mexicans
and the Blacks
alike.

I saw the boss turn and
walk back into his
office.

no sale.

Harry Keel turned and
began to walk to
the exit
carrying his shabby
briefcase.

I caught up to him at the
doorway.
tapped him on the
shoulder.

he turned and
saw me.

"Henry!"

"it's 'Hank,' Harry."

he stared.

"Jesus, what's happened to
you? you've
changed."

"you've changed too,
Harry."

"yeh."

we looked at each other
for a bit.

then he turned, opened
the door, walked out
and was
gone.

I walked back to my packing
table.

"hey, baby, who was your little
friend?" a Mexican girl
asked.

"nobody,
now
drop it!"

I ran a length of tape
along the top of the
packing box,
sealed it,

flipped it up onto the
finished pile in front of
me,
then walked back into
assembly to get a
new
light
fixture.

HOW DID THEY GET THEIR JOB?

a book reviewer has just called me a "second-rate Saroyan
with a hangover."
this is not so bad when you consider what some of my
women
have called me.

I have received many bad book reviews in my time and I
expect to receive
many more
but being human and like any other writer
I do get a bit galled when I feel that a reviewer has not
properly
done his homework
and when his critique is read by thousands of people
it tends to compound
misconception:

furthermore, a writer seldom gets to know his reviewer, I
mean
you don't get to see him sitting across from you, you
don't get to see the look of him, hear him talk, listen to
his ideas—

for only then would you know if that fine fellow is a
jack-off, a dinky moralist, a failed young writer or most
likely
just nothing at all.

but enough of that, tonight this second-rate Saroyan is
drinking his
way toward a first-rate hangover
not because of a crappy review but because it's just what
I like to do
while writing little stories and poems and sometimes
novels
influenced by
Hemingway, Céline, Dostoevsky, Turgenev, Jeffers,
Lawrence,
Cummings, Shostakovitch, Mahler, Mozart, Sibelius,
Beethoven,
Faulkner, Fante, Sherwood Anderson, Hamsun, my cats,
my wife,
the shape of my coat thrown over a chair, the weeping of
the planet,
the curving elbow of time, the flight of the hummingbird
and
Bartok in a dirty white apron handing me a plate of
shelled nuts.

PAPER AND PEOPLE

I should be thankful to have my own room to
type in
(and I am)
but it is a place of
absolute disarray—
books and magazines slide from
the bookcase,
letters received are sometimes
thrown into cartons but are often
just left on the floor
along with poems (mine and
theirs) amid week-old newspapers;
also canvases and paint tubes are
scattered here and there.

every day my readers
send me books of poems,
poetry magazines,
poetry manuscripts,
half-baked novels,
comic-books-in-progress from
hopeful young artists.

there are also old Racing Forms and
Programs everywhere.
there are too many calendars.
this desk is covered with empty
cigar boxes, used typewriter ribbons, mailing
labels, boxes of toothpicks and paper clips,
correction fluid, pencils, pens, bottle
openers, a can of household oil, cigarettes,
a discarded wristwatch, paint brushes, coins,
stamps, pocket combs, a stapling machine,

boxes of staples, gas bills, phone bills,
checkbook, Scotch tape, a cassette,
a woolen cap, a wooden Buddha, a cotton red devil,
7 or 8 books of matches, a typewriter, thumbtacks,
3 cigarette lighters, a bottle of India ink,
2 desk lamps, a radio, notepads, envelopes,
typing paper, bank statements, and under
all these things, many other things that
I would have to dig for to find.

but in the end
this desk, this room is, mostly, a mass of
PAPER; I just picked one up: a receipt from
the plumber dated 1981.
there is just too much PAPER everywhere and
the 5 drawers of this desk are also stuffed
with IT and I have no idea what most of it
means.

about once every two months I attempt to
clean this room, I fill trash bags with paper
and etc. until my desk and the floor are *almost*
clean
but then
more PAPER arrives,
more manuscripts from poets, more letters from
poets and others, more magazines, more more
more
I can't keep up with it all
and I wonder if anybody besides myself
has to keep fighting the arrival of floods of
PAPER?
I don't seem to have the time to keep up with
it and I wonder if other people
have this problem too?

I don't think so
because they seem to have nothing but time
to kill,
they don't seem to know what to do with themselves,
they
work crossword puzzles, play Scrabble, they
watch tv, they go visiting, go sit on
someone else's couch and talk for hours or they
visit museums or go to 3 movies a week. they
seem to have endless time to waste
and I have no time at all, I am fighting this
relentless tide of PAPER, all of which must be
gone through carefully because it often contains
notices from the IRS or unpaid bills.
yes, other people don't seem to have this
problem with PAPER PAPER PAPER gathering
everywhere, stacked upon itself,
and when people come to visit and
shoot my hours through the head they
offer nothing interesting or constructive.
I find myself resenting them and
their chatter
their idle ways
since I am always fighting for each minute,
a minute to straighten this out or that
out
and as I sit with them and their chatter,
as all the minutes are murdered,
I find that they are themselves like ACCUMULATED
PAPER,
you have to get rid of them
before they overwhelm and smother you.

am I the only one with this
problem?

PAPER and PEOPLE, such a waste,
such a terrible
waste.

WRITER'S BLOCK

the typewriter sits silent, it's as if you've
been betrayed, it's as if a murder has
occurred.
yet words still run through your brain:
"the Spanish bird sings!"
what can
that mean?
at least it's a ripple, even if unusable.

when will the keys
beat into the
paper
again?
it's so easy to die long before the
fact of it.

I look at the machine resting under its black
cover; an unpaid gas bill sleeps on top of
it.

there is a small refrigerator in the
room, it makes the only audible sound
here.

I open it and look inside:
it's empty.

I sit back down in the chair and wait; then I
decide to fool the
typewriter.

I write this
now
with a ballpoint
pen
in a red
notebook;
I am sneaking up on a poem;
there will soon be something for that
frigging
typewriter
to do!

there is a French expression, "without
literature
life is hell."

the glory and power of that!

now let the Spanish bird sing!

DISORDER AND EARLY SORROW

I was in the habit of sleeping there in the
nearby abandoned graveyard,
two or three mornings a week,
whenever I experienced my worst morning hangovers
and
just didn't feel like going right back to the
neighborhood bar where I spent my
afternoons and evenings.

it was cool and quiet
there in the tall wet grass in that
graveyard;
the small insects didn't crawl on

you as they did when you lay
in the dry itchy
summer grass.
sleep was more possible.

and always before sleeping
I'd look around the graveyard, at the tilting
headstones, their inscriptions obscured,
tilting at
very strange angles, having finally succumbed
to the law of gravity.
(here were the truly forgotten dead
and I felt I wanted to join them.)
the old rusty wrought iron fence
that surrounded the
graveyard seemed more to sag than
tilt,
the quiet was utterly
marvelous,
and there was nobody about but the forgotten
dead,
and I wondered about their bones
buried there,
bones having long ago escaped from the
rotting coffins.
it was all so curious,
so strange,
those long dead and forgotten
bones,
those lives gone, totally
erased, their history now never to be
recorded.

I felt sad for those lost lives
and felt

there was a perspective to
be gleaned about it all
but it was a vague one,
one only partially
understood.

I was usually awakened
with the noon sun
burning my upturned face
and I would rise,
not looking back at my faceless
companions,
and make my way
back to the bar.

then to sit there and look down
into my first draft
beer, wondering about things:
the forgotten dead,
a fly,
the bartender's shirt,
voices emanating from those sitting
nearby,
the smell of urine from the
crapper,
the sound of passing automobiles,
somebody laughing,
my trembling hand lighting a first
cigarette.

nothing to do then but
get drunk
again.

IN THIS PLACE

there are the dead, the deadly and the dying.
there is the cross, the builders of the cross and the
burners of the
cross.

the pattern of my life forms like a cheap shadow
on the wall before me.

my love
what is left of it
now must crawl
to wherever it can crawl.

the strongest know that death is
final
and the happiest are those gifted with the
shortest journey.

THE UNINITIATED

I was drinking with this fellow the other
night, not a bad sort, young but not a bad
sort, compared to some others.
I live an isolated life, don't mind that, prefer
that,
but now and then
(mostly then)
I don't drink alone.

it went all right.
we exchanged a few sad tales about
women.
we had some good laughs.

then he got a bit
intoxicated.
he bent forward, grinning
slyly, said,
"come on now, you got to admit you probably
miss the good times you had on
skid row, on the bum, on the road, all
that."

it's when a fellow talks that
way, even if he's not a bad
sort, you know he's never been
anywhere.

not that you have to have been there
but if you were
and once you get out
almost everything that happens after that
seems blessed.

"no," I told him, "I don't miss skid
row."

"ah, come on," he said, "cut out the
shit!"

"you better ease up on the drinks,"
I told him. "you've got a lot to
learn
and an even longer way to
go."

CICADA

writers love to use the word
"cicada" in a poem.
it makes them believe that
they are there, that they
have done it.
every time I see this word
in a poem, I think, damn
it, haven't the editors
caught on yet?
that it's a con?
a way to milk the game?

and look at me:
here I'm using it:
"cicada."

well, that means that
this poem surely will get
published.

see?

it works.

NEVER INTERRUPT A WRITER AT WORK

most simply don't understand that writing is
done
at a certain time and in a certain
place.
we work just like other professional
people
like
dentists
doctors
butchers
lawyers
fry cooks
policemen
actors
trapeze artists
waiters
taxi drivers, airline pilots, insurance salesmen,
bond bailsmen, auto
mechanics and sundry
others.

we need our quiet time to do what we are supposed
to do.
it's as simple and profound and
necessary as
that.

and you're absolutely right
if you think I'm bitching
about you
about this.

OH MY

very painful to write this
of course
but most poets are just big
tit-suckers:
accepting readings
taking university chairs
praying for tenure
writing books on poetic
technique and
giving
lectures.

very painful to write this
of course
but hardly as painful
as
attempting to read
their
Selected
Works.

having said the above
there goes
my last chance
to join their
worldwide
circle
jerk.

MEETING THEM

meeting the talented and famous
is almost always
disappointing.
they usually seem rather common,
even dull.
of course, they are
(at the time of meeting)
out of character,
out of their creative
element.

there must be a
pause
of course,
a time to relax,
the flame can only
be turned up
at given
moments,
otherwise
they'd burn
out.

yet
when you meet them
you still
look for
a sign,
a hint
of their
magnetism and
talent.
but there usually is
none.

how close we all are
to being
nothing
most of the
time

and
for some of us
nothing
all of the
time.

NO EULOGIES, PLEASE

I don't want anybody
at my funeral
saying:

"he was really a
good guy, after
all—"

some
jackass
making some stupid
remarks about my
worth or lack of
same.

rather than some
jackass
spouting off

it would be
nice

if one of my
x-ladies was
there
wearing too much makeup
dressed in
high heels and a
tight green
dress
saying
"he was really a
great fuck,
after all."

of course
she won't be
there
and it won't
happen
because
I never
was.

FINALITY

mad,
Ezra Pound
the
traitor
dragged through the streets of Italy in a wooden cage.

mad,
Ezra
at
the
end

saying,
"All that I have written is worth nothing."

the
immortal
soul
finally
understanding
itself
at
last,
always
knows

that.

THE MACHINERY OF LOSS

sitting here, sneezing
god-damned cold coming on
lost at the track today
they sent in a string of long shots that
should have been shot in the head and
buried
long ago.

too many of my poems have been created
only in response to
losses such as this.

of late, I've preferred writing only when
I'm feeling good.

good or very
good, it
doesn't matter.

and when there's nothing to write
about
one writes about
writing.

it's as natural as dropping your
shorts.

I'm a writer who has had a bad day
at the track
and maybe coming down with the
flu
sitting here in slippers and
walking shorts
listening to disco music on the
radio

but all the time
the brain cells are throbbing
working on a new system
to get at those four-legged
motherfuckers.

meanwhile, sitting at the typer,
doing these finger exercises
I keep the rest home and madhouse
at bay.

read this to your class in contemporary
literature and tell them how easy it
is.

then send those children out to walk
the asphalt like the rest
of us.

PART TWO

there's a lioness
down the hallway

put on your lion's mask
and wait.

DAMSELS OF THE NIGHT

at first I believed
that those 3 a.m. taps on the window
were a delightful miracle,
and I would
let some night creature in
off the boulevard
with a cheerful "hello there!"
and she would respond
with some brisk joke
then she'd move
uneasily about,
looking into the refrigerator,
opening and closing drawers,
making odd conversational observations,
then finally use the
bathroom.

I would sit with one damsel
or another
night after night and
they were all of similar stripe and
there would be
smoking and
quiet talk
some laughter
but there was seldom any
sex, and then only at
some wild suggestion of
theirs.

most left before noon
and I'd make ready to sleep
again

thinking of them
sitting there
combing their hair,
talking,
smiling,
gesturing,
swallowing a pill
now and then.

I was never sure
what the damsels really
wanted
or why they came
to visit me
and as their 3 a.m. visits
continued,
some of the miracle
wore thin;
in fact, there were times
when the damsels made
stupid and vicious demands
or even threats
as if I was in debt
to them in return
for their very
existence.

they were fair ladies—all
if you didn't look too
close
and if you
did
you saw faces
hard and brutal as an
ax,

beyond compassion,
beyond any real interest in men,
beyond their own female natures,
their vulnerability long ago
extinguished.

I tried not to look too
close,
only allowing myself to be
superficially aware of their bodies,
their hair,
their clothes,
their smiles,
and even
their colorful street
lingo.

the vulnerable ones
not yet hardened by the streets
(if there ever were any such)
seldom if ever
knocked
and if they did
I was so used to the others
so used to
the women who were
tough to the core
that I didn't recognize
the difference
and I suppose
if there were any still vulnerable
I discouraged them
with my indifference
while
the shrews grimly hung
on.

still, you know, each time
there was a tap
at the
window
and a strange damsel
entered in a
rush,
with a burst of cheap perfume,
with her
high heels clicking
on the floor,
a bright joke on her
red lips,
sent to visit by one of her
sisters of the street,
I could not help but
wonder, will this one
be different?

but
within minutes
I'd realize
that this one
was no
different
and
I'd go on and
play the game
anyhow,
sit and smoke and
listen until
noon
when a reality would enter
that was much harder
more relentless

than they were
and they would leave
before the force of it
became too obvious
those
damsels of the night
and I'd go back to
bed, alone,
gladly
alone,
thinking,
the next poor
son-of-a-bitch
is going to have to
be satisfied with
what just
left.

FOREWARNED

dear Hank, I'm still in Wisconsin
but I'm coming soon
to spend some time with
you.
don't get me wrong, I don't want
your money, I don't want to know
how you made it as a writer
or to help me with my writing,
I don't want to bother you or
waste your time, I just want to
sit down and talk to you.
I have so much in my heart to say.
is this asking too much?

so maybe you could call
your publisher and tell
them that when
Roberta calls
to give her your phone number.
I hope you and all
the cats are fine.
I'm really looking forward
to finally meeting you in
the flesh!
love,

SHE LOST WEIGHT

my roommate Kristyn lost weight, *she tells me,*
she used to weigh 175 pounds
and then she lost 40 pounds and realized
suddenly that she was
attractive. I shared this apartment
with her and she started fucking
black guys. she went to
work before I did
and I'd get up in the morning
and here'd be some black guy standing
there with an Afro that reached
halfway across the room. jesus,
I wouldn't even know his
name and there was a different one
each morning.
finally one morning one of them was
ripping her off. he's carrying out
her TV set and her camera and
her radio and her stereo

and then he starts on what's left
and I tell him, just a minute, brother,
that stuff is mine. you keep your hands
off *my* crap!
o.k., baby, he says.

I had to move out, *she tells me*.
when Kristyn weighed 175 pounds
she was no trouble, she had the
nicest personality, then she lost all that
weight and got god-damned
paranoid, popping pills and screaming
and wearing my panties,
I tell you, I had to get away from that
bitch!

MILITARY SURPLUS

my wife is more apprehensive than I am
and we were in a surplus store
poking around when
my wife said, "I want two gas
masks."

"gas masks?"

"yes, there are all those storage tanks
nearby and if they explode there is
going to be nothing but flame and
gas!"

"I never thought about that," I
said.

my wife found a clerk and sure enough he
took us to the gas masks—ugly, unwieldy

stupid-looking things.
the clerk showed us how they
operated.

"we'll take two," my wife
said.

we walked to the counter to pay.

"do you have gas masks for cats?" my wife
asked. "we have 5 cats."

"cats?" the clerk asked.

"yes, what will the cats do if there is an
explosion?"

"lady, cats are different than we are, they
are of a lower order."

"I think cats are better than we are,"
I put in.

the clerk looked at me. "we don't have
gas masks for cats."

"do you accept MasterCard?" I
asked.

"yes," he said.

the clerk took my card, swiped it, wrote
up the slip, handed it to me.

I
signed it.

"do you have any cats?" my wife asked
him.

"I have children," he said.

"our cats are our children," my wife
said.

the clerk bagged the masks, handed them to
me.
"do you have any size
eleven-and-one-half sneakers?" I asked.

"no, sir."

we walked out of there.

and the clerk didn't even
thanks us for
our
business.

A DIFFICULT WOMAN

I remember once sitting in a hotel
room when my woman came in drunk and said,
"Christ, I couldn't hold it, I had to piss in the
elevator!"
I was drunk too, I was barefoot and just wearing
my shorts.
I got up and walked out the door and down
the hall and pushed the elevator
button.
it came up.
the door opened.
the elevator was empty but sure enough
there in the corner was the
puddle.
as I was standing there a man and a
woman came out of their room

and walked to the
elevator.
the door was beginning to close
so I held it open with my hand
so they could get
on.
as the door began to close I heard the
woman say,
"that man was in his shorts."
and just as it closed I heard the man say,
"and he pissed in the elevator!"

I went back to my room and told her,
"they think *I* pissed in the elevator!"

"who?" she asked.

"some people."

"what people?"

"the people who saw me standing there
in my shorts."

"well, screw them!" she said.

she sat there quietly drinking a glass
of wine.

"take a bath," I said.

"you take a bath," she said.

"at least take a shower," I said.

"you take a shower," she said.

I sat down and poured myself a glass of
wine.

we were always arguing about
something.

TALK

"A and K have split. K, he's filing for the
divorce and living with M out in the
Valley.

H left G, she still has the kids and he's
going to school, he only has a year to go
to get his B.A.

S and R are still together.
and so are L and W.

B went up north and N was to follow
but she decided not to and then she told him
it was over. B really loves their kid, it's
too bad.

C and L still have troubles but they talk
everything out, they want to make it
work.

so do D and F. they got married and she went
to New York City for 5 months to study
dancing.

oh, G is in New York City too, studying drama.
she got that money from the insurance co.
after the car crash.

I think it's good that people keep trying,
that they talk things out.
they're not like *you*. the moment something goes
wrong you walk right out the door, you won't talk,
you're ready to dump me and everything else *forever*!
Jesus
Christ, when things are worth keeping I think
they're worth *talking* about! two people living

together, it's kind of an *obligation*, don't you
see? actually it's more than an obligation, it's a holy
communion.
hey! where the hell are you *going*? what's the
matter *now*? *hey!* you son-of-a-bitch!"

WHERE THE ACTION IS REAL

this is where we live
down at Prairie and Century Blvds.
the gamblers the hustlers the lovers the
pimps
all those
who think they know.

boy, what a party! and after it's over
we'll all go home and drink Cutty Sark
in air-conditioned flats.

the dwarf rushes by and makes his way to
the ten-dollar window
knocking a paper cup of coffee out of a
young girl's hand. she's small and
thin and her T-shirt reads:
GRAB AND FONDLE, THEN PAY! she has no
breasts.

I was $118 ahead at the end of the 3rd race.
now I am $140 down. I go to take a piss.
I wash my hands. I even wash my face.
(*watch* me, you back in that trash bin
fulla monkeys!) I don't comb my hair:
I feel silly looking into mirrors. I
go buy a sandwich. I bite into it. I
have begun to hate meat. it stinks like

carrion. I don't understand it. but
everybody eats it. I force the sandwich
down.

I am standing there and just like in a
movie, here comes one of those
tall sexy slim ones, working the crowd,
young and dizzy in a long dress like they
wear now but with a slit running up one
leg, almost to the hip (light or dark meat,
almost everybody eats it). well, I
understand what's behind all that display: pleasure
and trouble. anyhow, ho hum,
she leans up against me, giving me
flank and a dubious nudge of breast, she makes
me feel like a fucking fool and she says to me,
"lemmee see . . ." and I say, "see what?" and she
says, "your program, mister, your *program.*"
I hand it to her. she spills some of her drink on
my shirt. she smiles. then she hands the program back.
she runs toward a window. I watch her ass. shit
drops out of that. just like out of mine.

then we see something else.
it's the last race and
the #6 horse and the #8 horse are
eleven lengths out, no chance at
all. then the #6 stumbles and tumbles
into the #8. the jocks go down in a
crash of horse craziness.
two little men in silk
with the hearts of giants.
such pretty silks
such tiny asses and legs and arms
now sprawled on the sod.

(the noisy ambulance appears
but it does not seem to be in
a hurry.)
the horses are up but
the jocks are very still
in the California sun
as the winning number goes up
on the tote

and the 9 race card is
finished for the
day.

ACADEMY AWARD?

I sit with my daughter and my girlfriend
in a Westwood Village movie house.
the movie has gotten rave reviews
but as it continues
each scene is predictable
it's just one long pedestrian platitude
but the audience is enjoying
it
and I am thinking
o my god
there is still an hour and
15 minutes left.
I say to my daughter and
girlfriend:
"listen, do you really think we
should stay?"
"well, if you like it," says my
daughter.

"yes, if you like it," says my
girlfriend.
"I was only staying because I
thought you both liked it,"
I say.
"I was staying for the same reason,"
says my daughter.
"likewise," says my girlfriend.
we get up and walk out of
there.
it is such a splendid moment:
there is no law that we have to
stay—
they have our money
but we have escaped an hour and
15 minutes of
trying to get our money's
worth.
the movie
a tragic historical depiction
of the 1930s
will probably win an
Academy Award
but the car looks so very good
in the parking lot
and driving off we laugh about
it
again and again
as if we had seen a very good
comedy
which is exactly what tragedy
becomes
when it's badly done.

BEACH BOYS

only the young go to the beach now.
I have a good body for my age
bull neck and chest
and powerful legs.
but my back is badly scarred
from a former malady.
I feel some shame for my deformity
and I would not go there
to the beach
only my woman insists
and if she has the courage to go there
with me
then I must have the courage to go there
with her.

but I wonder where the old and the crippled
and the ugly are?
shouldn't the beaches welcome them too?
where are the one-legged people?
the deformed?
the armless?

I watch the young boys on their surfboards
slim strong bodies gliding.

some of them will end up in the madhouse
some of them will gain 80 pounds
some of them will commit suicide
most of them will eventually stop coming to the
beach.

and there is the sun and there is the sand
as the young boys zoom down palisades of water
as the eager young girls watch them and wait.

the young girls are thoughtless and very pleased with
themselves.

I stretch out
turn on my stomach
close my eyes
and then suddenly they
all are
gone.

I'M NO GOOD

she writes me that she is homeless
now.

how ironic, I think, that
this lady, this highly paid
female executive
who lived in the
Hollywood Hills,
who drove an expensive new car
and who invited a drunken slob
(me) to share her bed,
this lady who had her own
office,
her own staff,
this lady who traveled
all over the world,
this lady who discovered musical talent
and promoted it,
this lady who had celebrities
vie to attend her parties
is now homeless.
"I'm used to it now," she

writes, "it no longer bothers
me."

it is a two-page letter.
I read it, fold it up, put it in
a drawer and don't
reply.

I am as cold as the world.
if it doesn't bother her, it
doesn't bother me.

I get on my exercise bike,
begin pumping away while
listening to
Wagner.

this is the way she'd like to
remember me, I'm
sure.

FRIEND OF THE FAMILY

she told me:
when I was a little girl I was taken to see
an eye doctor.
it was dark in there and he told me
to hold something.
I did.
it was soft.
then it started getting hard.
I heard the doctor breathing.
I thought it was part of the examination.
I didn't know.

but I also felt that something was
terribly wrong.
he kept me in there a long time
and told me to keep holding the
instrument.
when he was finished he
turned on the lights.
my mother was in the waiting
room.
I didn't know what to do.
the doctor was a friend of the
family, a good friend.
he'd been over to dinner.
he gave me some candy and
took me out to see my
mother.
"she's just fine," he told my
mother, "she passed the
examination."
"oh, thank you, Harry,"
she said.
then she took me out of
the office and we walked away
down the hall.
I unwrapped the candy
and put it in my
mouth.

"isn't the doctor a nice
man?" my mother
asked.
"yes," I said.

but the candy tasted musty
and stale

and for some
strange reason
I feared my mother then
as I learned to hate the
doctor.

SOLVING A CRIME BEFORE IT BEGINS

perhaps of all of them she would have been
considered the most
beautiful.
but, like all of us, she had one small
flaw,
and her flaw—
or it seemed to be a flaw to me—
was that she *loved Sherlock Holmes*.
I mean, that fellow who solves all those
mysteries and goes on
solving them forever!
over time
we saw all the Sherlock Holmes
movies (more than once)
and all his TV shows
(again and again).
I didn't quite understand what was
so intriguing about S.H.

"you're kidding me?" I asked.
"you're joking?"

a beautiful body, a beautiful
face, a fair mind except for . . . that.

"I'm *not* joking," she said firmly.

and right there I knew that I
could never live with that
woman.
not that Sherlock Holmes
was all that
terrible,
only I knew that her obsession
was a clue perhaps to
other things that
lurked within her
far more terrible than
her love for
Sherlock Holmes.
I could feel
something dark
lurking within
her.

you're unfair and cruel,
I can hear you say, doesn't
everybody have a right to
innocent choices and feelings?

of course, and my choice
and my gut feeling was to
get the hell out of there,
Watson, and
fast,
leaving that unsettling
unsolved mystery
for the
next
guy.

NOTE FOR MY WALL

it's no good
after all.
it has been cut in half
drawn and
quartered and
hung out to dry.

it was hardly good
even when it was good.

the ego gets caught
in a web of desire
the ego creates that strange mirage,
love.

I need a new home for my ego.
who will she be
this time?

THE WINE THAT ROARED

we'd get drunk and she'd start in
again about her son: "I don't know, he
doesn't write me, I haven't seen
him for 5 years, maybe I'll never
see him again!" she'd be
crying and
dropping ashes on her skirt, the
wine red on her
lips.
"who?" I'd ask, "who ya talkin'
about?"
"Billy-Boy, Billy-Boy, my son!"

I'd get up and pace the floor
in my underwear.
she was ten years older than I was
and we'd been shacked for 2
years.
"listen," I'd say, "every time
you get drunk you crank up
about your Billy-Boy!"
"I may never see Billy-Boy
again! I put him through
college, now he won't speak
to me!" she'd say.
I'd spin around, my cigarette
glowing in the darkened room.
"listen, you whore, show me
some leg! now!
hike up your skirt!
there!
that's good, that's better!
I've been working
like a dog all week,
waiting for the weekend, and hell,
you're no fun talkin' all the time
about your Billy-Boy!
I'm your man now!
I'm a tiger!
look at these arms!
look at these legs!
look at my chest!
I can kick ASS!"

she'd lift her drink and
smile, "yeah, you're good,
especially your legs, you
have great legs, Hank!"

"thanks, whore."

I'd go and sit down, look at her
a second time.

"now, hike up your skirt a
little higher! there!
there!
ya know, you're lucky to
be living with me.
drink up!"

she would.
then I'd walk over, splash her
glass full again
with the mad red
wine.
I'd pour myself another one,
drain the entire glass, pour
another, stare down at
her.

"you just don't appreciate who you're
living with!"

she'd sigh.
"I can't help it if I think of
Billy-Boy once in a while, Hank,
he's my son!"

I'd smash my wine glass
against the wall then.
"damn it, you're no FUN!
all right, ALL RIGHT!
we'll find your friggin' Billy-Boy
and I'LL KICK HIS
ASS!"

we'd drink on then for maybe 3 or 4 more
hours.

and the next Monday I'd be back at
Sears Roebuck, the good stock boy,
pushing my cart
around, supplying the counters
and the clerks with their needed
goods
wondering if I'd have to search the
bars that night to find her,
to dig her out of there.

it was some life.
loyal sons-of-bitches like me didn't come
along too often, maybe
never.

no, there was no
maybe
about it.
they just never come
along.

2:07 A.M.

Hank, how are you doing?

it's like sucking seaweed out of a rabbit
hutch.

that doesn't make
sense.

all I know is that things are going like they've
never gone before.

you could be suffering from delusions.

that's what makes it so difficult.

you need exercise. have you been drinking your orange juice in the mornings?

yes, and I'm taking long walks in the evening.

I'm happy for you. I miss you.

you're good to me. I want to thank you.

sometimes I miss you so much. it's like a big hole in my life.

smoke a cigarette, it'll go away.

how much have you had to drink tonight?

very little.

how many bottles do you have there?

three.

three?

yes, three.

are you going to drink all of them?

probably.

you know what that will do to you?

yes.

you know how it hurts me?

yes.

you know how unfair it is to me?

yes . . .

then why do you do it?

I don't know.

do you love me?

I hate to answer questions like that.
I never ask you
questions.

but you do.

sure, like, what time is it? or, how is your mother?

why don't you ask more questions? what's wrong with
asking
questions?

I just don't like to do it.

you're getting drunk now.

yes.

do you have to drink all 3 bottles now?

I think so.

see, you've *answered* a question!

yes, I have . . .

so, you see . . .

oh, Jesus Christ! please don't
keep phoning and talking all night. I've
got to sleep.

all right.

but don't take your phone off the
hook.

all right, but can't you
say something nice to me now?

ummmm . . .

say something.

look, baby, I've got to make the track tomorrow.

the track?

yes.

she screams and hangs the
phone up.

she'll phone back.

if she doesn't
I'll phone her.

but it *is*
like sucking seaweed out of a rabbit
hutch.

there have been other
times when it wasn't like that
other times when I thought that maybe . . .

but you'll have to
excuse me now, the phone's
ringing.

A CLEAN, WELL-LIGHTED PLACE

the old fart, he used his literary reputation
to reel them in one at a time,
each younger than the last.
he liked to meet them for luncheon and
wine
and he'd talk and listen to them
talk.
whatever wife or girlfriend he had at the moment
was made to
understand that this sort of thing made him
feel "young again."
and when the luncheons became more
than luncheons
the young ladies vied to bed down with
this
literary
genius.
in between, he continued to write,
and late at night in his favorite bar
he liked to talk about writing and his amorous
adventures.
actually, he was just a drunk
who liked young ladies,
writing itself,
and talking about writing.
it wasn't a bad life.
it was certainly more interesting than
what most men were
doing.
at one time he was probably the
most famous writer in the
world.

many tried to write like he did
drink like he did
act like he did
but he was the original.
then life began to
catch up with him.
he began to age quickly.
his large bulk began to wither.
he was growing old
before his time.
finally it got to where he couldn't
write anymore,
"it just wouldn't come"
and the psychiatrists couldn't
do anything for him but only
made it worse.
then he took his own cure,
early one morning,
alone
just as his father had done
many years
before.

a writer who can't write any
more is dead
anyhow.
he knew that.
he knew that what he was
killing was already
dead.

and then the critics
and the hangers-on
and the publicists
and his heirs
moved in
like vultures.

DO WE REALLY CARE?

she was a pain on the set, a huge
pain, she demanded script changes,
argued with the director,
fought with
the other actors, arrived hours late (some
say drunk or drugged) and when her
contract expired she was let
go.
she complained that she had been
"knifed."
she went back to her mansion and took to
her bed, eating nothing but sweets.
she ate incessantly with all
the curtains drawn.
her husband, a successful actor,
insisted he loved her still.
to prove it, he married her once
again in a special ceremony.
her original wedding
gown no longer fit so
she was beautifully refitted
but after the second marriage she went
back to bed and resumed eating.
once again
the pounds multiplied and
that only depressed her more.
soon even the scandal sheets forgot
her.
months went by.
then suddenly she appeared on a magazine
cover.
she had made a comeback.

she was still fat, fatter than ever
but she had dyed her hair
blonde and had it cut in a
trendy style.
"I am back," she said.
she was hired for a new TV series.
the first week of shooting went
well.
then she started coming in hours
late (some say drunk, some say
drugged, some say both).
she argued with the writers, the
actors and the
director.
within two weeks
she was fired and the series was
junked.
she went back to bed, drew the
curtains, and began eating
again.
her husband was soon seen at functions
with a girl 30 years his
junior.
back at the mansion his wife
fired the servants,
hired new ones
and purchased a
German shepherd she called
"Marco."
she and Marco lay on
the bed and spent the days
eating sweets together,
their favorite being

dark chocolates
with the juicy
red cherries
inside.

FOR CRYING OUT LOUD

weeping women
over dinner
crying into the soup.

weeping women
in motorcars
complaining.

weeping women
on the telephone.

weeping women
crying from the
treetops.

weeping women
rattling mens' hearts
inside of paper bags.

weeping women
leaping 30 feet
into the air

demanding love
more and more
love.

I'd gladly give them
more love

if they weren't
so demanding

if they'd only
let it
rest awhile.

you can love
love to death
until there's
nothing left
but a
wristbone.

then finally you're
compelled to
start over with
another
somebody.

HIGH SCHOOL GIRLS

the girls used to say to me: "you're so
negative!"
they said this to me in a very final sense and
it seemed to satisfy
them.
(the boys didn't say anything at all to me because
I was usually angry and they didn't
dare.)
but the girls were very vocal and very sure,
saying, "you're so
negative!"

it made them feel intellectual, or,
at least, intelligent.
they had already formed opinions
about what life was
and about what life should be
and how one should perform
in this life.

it was all right with me, I didn't want to be
liked by them, I didn't want to fuck them or
marry them or
even date them.
I found none of them
beautiful.

now, 50 years later,
I find that almost every elderly female is
negative
and I'm positive
and I'm still glad I didn't fuck, marry or
date any of them then.
they, now of advanced age, have
largely become
sad, embittered and even
psychotic.

I guess because they started
so positive
so early
it just all wore
out.
and that's the end of the whole amusing
story.

EMERGENCY

"in case of accident
please get in touch with
Henry Chinaski.
there is a very good chance
that you will find him at
the racetrack (whichever
one is running)."

along with various addresses
and phone numbers
she always carries this message
in her wallet
along with her I.D.

I find this particularly
enchanting,
even more so
when she says,
"I love you, poo-poo . . ."

her pet name just for me,
I hope.

FOR A WOMAN WHO MIGHT SOME DAY BECOME A NUN:

she writes me from Paris
with a forwarding address in Athens
that she did not join the missionaries,
which is good,
I'd hate to waste such great
stuff,

poets need meat
with their wine,
and if she blows
into my place
smoking a Dutch cigar
I'll have to show her
a few tricks
I learned from a Spanish whore
in a small room over a bar
outside the Plaza Monumental
de Tijuana
the afternoon Capetillo
Orauna and Rosas
were on.

then,
we'll discuss
Rimbaud.

SOME PEOPLE ASK FOR IT

he fell in love with a famous
opera star
and attended her performances
and wrote her long love letters
to which she did not reply.

she was famous.
he was not.

after some years her
talent declined
while his compositions
began to be played.

they met and soon thereafter
they
married.

she was older.
she began to drink
and
sang no longer.
she slowly
went mad
while his fame grew.

he continued to live
with her. he was quietly
homosexual.

finally
nothing worked for him except
his music.

once after an argument
he stood barefoot
in the river
on a freezing night
hoping to catch
pneumonia and die.

he didn't.

sometime later
she sold his love letters
for booze
and created a scandal.
so you see
their love
it wasn't entirely wasted
after all.

but I think
he should have either stuck
with young boys
or found a better way
to kill himself.

AGAINST THE WINDOW PANE

you're always demanding a
new me.

you're sitting on the couch now,
complaining.

your voice scratches
against the window pane.

I think that no matter
what we've done to each
other (and neither of us
has been fair)

that it is your tone of voice
that is finally most unfair.

all of our betrayals
yours and mine
don't deserve that tone of
voice.

or
that dark wailing
face

so sure that the next man
will not treat you
the way I did

or that you will not treat him
the way you did me.

your voice scratches against the
window pane

and
nothing in life ever changes
and I want to tell you so
now.

AN ANSWER TO A DAY'S WORTH OF MAIL:

dear Mr. C: I admire your writing
and I'd like to come by sometime
bring a 6-pack and talk.
dear Mr. C: your writing makes me
strong and I'd like to bring
a 6-pack and talk. I write poems
too.
dear Mr. C: I consider you one of
the finest poets of the decade,
perhaps one of the finest poets
ever born. I'd like to bring over
a bottle and talk to you.
dear Mr. C: I have always liked
your writing. I will be passing
through your city in June and I'll
have my wife with me. she's very sexy
and I think she's in love with
you.

dear Sirs: I can't see any of you
except for the one with the sexy
wife. when you come over she must

be wearing high-heeled shoes,
a short skirt, nylons,
be a little drunk, must prefer
Turgenev to Chekhov, must have on
green earrings and must not be in-
clined to fart when startled. her tits
needn't be gigantic. and,
to the rest of you
gentlemen, I wish to thank you all for
admiring my endeavors
literary.
    Chinaski.

NEW YORK, NEW YORK

he was on the hall telephone
saying, "darling, if you don't
come back to me, I'm going
to kill myself!
I swear it!"

I passed him on the way
to my room which was
upstairs.
he was the neighborhood poet.
he had on a silk scarf, a
beret,
wore a goatee and had a
pigtail.

it was 9 a.m.
but I was already
tired.
I got up to my room

and stretched out on the
bed.

there was a man who was
going to kill himself if his
woman left him.
I hadn't had a woman
for 3 years and I was
24 years
old.

I thought, I am missing out
on something.

then I got off of the bed,
walked to the dresser and
opened a bottle of
wine.
I poured out a glassful.
I drank it,
put the bottle away,
went to the
door, locked it behind me
and
went back down the
stairway.

the man was no longer
there.
I stood and looked at the
telephone.
I had nobody to
phone.

I walked back out on
the street.
it was crowded

as the people walked
back and
forth.

I chose a direction
and walked in that
direction.
I walked into the first
bar I saw,
sat down.
I ordered a beer,
had a hit
and then suddenly it came to
me:
that man hadn't been
talking to anybody
on the telephone.
I don't know how I
knew it
but I
knew.

son-of-a-bitch, I
thought, I've got to get
out of Greenwich Village
before I get like
him!

and I did.

THE KNIFE WALTZ

they leave you alone
looking at the walls;
you chain-smoke
cigarettes
and pour whiskey into
your shredded gut,
you know the
feeling and the
result—
another
ten-round bout in hell.

but
you've done the same thing
to them
people simply are not good
to one
another.

yes,
I deserve this
evening
as I have deserved many
similar evenings
and now I'm depressed
and finally out of
music
hope
and
cigarettes.

DUSTY SHOES

the women that I have left behind grow fat, listless, age
rapidly, they coarsen, are embittered and some just finally
die alone
but the living still often think of me
with some regret
with some longing
now realizing that I made the nights and the days
electric for them
like it had never been and
that even asleep after making love
they rested and dreamed better than
ever before.

it didn't matter that
I caused them consternation in odd places like
drug stores, parks, elevators, laundromats, airports,
doctors' offices, restaurants and in many other
places.

I was funny, I was strange, I was not quite
right.
I puzzled those ladies, sometimes made them angry
often delighted them,
kept them interested
in things
and I was difficult to keep
around:
"hey! where are you going? you
just got here!"

after me, there was nobody for them.

some of them knew it right away.

with others it took months and with a few,
years.

I wasn't really a lady's man, I was just an aberration
with the ability to transcend the
ordinary; I was unshaven with dusty shoes, wrinkled
shirt, crushed
pants
but
I brought something to each one of them that
they had never ever experienced before
and when I took it away
new men, travel, parties, weekends, concerts,
meals, beds, books, pictures, days, nights, movies, TV,
etc.
all those things lost their edge,
became dull, more ordinary,
less satisfying.

it was, I fear,
a truly difficult experience
for them to attempt to
go on living without
me.

I wouldn't want to try
it.

VULGAR POEM

listening to medieval organ music
on the radio while
sitting at this machine.

there is a letter from a girl
at Vassar
at my elbow.
she writes that she is

doing a paper on me:
"Vulgar Literature."

she remarks that
most serious
writers are not so
terribly vulgar
and then comes the usual
question: why do you
write like you
do?

I always try to answer
that question a different
way
each time it's asked,
only this time the question
had been prefaced by a
certain assumption
so that there was
a second implied question:
why are you so
vulgar
when most serious
writers are
not?

well, right now
I'm sitting here typing
my poems
and it's something
to do in the
evening
rather than just
laying on the couch and
looking at the wall.

I'm quite comfortable
quite pleased
right now
sitting in my shorts
with
nobody around.
I like that.

to me
there's no agony
no struggle
as I write
no loneliness and
no vulgarity
that I know of.

I don't suffer
serious artistic cramps
getting these words down
although you
may suffer reading them.

and I really don't think
there are that
many good writers around
right now,
serious or not.

I am sent countless books
unasked
through the mail
written
by the supposed premier
writers of our time.

when I have trouble going
to sleep at night

I tell my girlfriend,
"please pass me
one of those books
written by
a Master."

"which one?"
she asks.

"it doesn't matter,"
I tell her.

I begin reading.
I can't get through more
than 2 or 3 pages
before the weariness
descends.

the book falls
to the floor and
I am barely able to
reach over and
turn off the lamp.

as long as the world
is full of so many
serious writers
I'll never have
insomnia.

I'm proud, however, that
my work is considered to be
"Vulgar Literature"
by some lady at Vassar!

not to change the
subject but
one of my 3 cats

just
puked on the floor
and I had to put it
out into the
rain.

and I won $400
at the track
today
so I'm somewhat
pleased.
(I've been playing
the horses for
43 years:
it's for the want
of anything else
reasonable to
do.)

(so why don't I
paint instead? go to museums?
travel? take a cooking
class? clean up my
act?)

on the radio there's
more organ music
now.
I like it,
dark and heavy sounds
like the rain.

I can feel blood,
murder and madness swirling
everywhere.

it's a fine night

filling this glass
again and again
with
thick
red
wine.

some are good at
cleaning the shit stains
out of the toilet;
others at
polishing the mirror
of their own vanity;
many are expert
at composing inoffensive
verse
or
sucking dick.

but while the drippings from
their thin minds
spill from their tongue

I'll continue to
type.

THIS ONE

this one's
well-read
tells amusing stories of the homeless and
millionaires.
she's Greek
false teeth
lives with her millionaire, washes
my dishes, cuts
my toenails, doesn't pretend to be a
writer.
she's read everything, laughs more than
most, has been in the madhouse
twice, gives incisive instructions because
I am
idiotic, can't even pick newspapers up off the floor—
they become yellowed and
I read the same headlines
over and over
as I walk about.
we both drink
she turns the radio up too high
I bear it
at least it's classical.

I tell her how difficult it is to be a
writer: to
awaken at 11:30 a.m.
sick and puking
brain frazzled and drained
and hanging there in front
white blob of gut never touched by a
maiden's
hand.

we go somewhere
I sit with 6 cans of Fresca
sweating out the booze
sign my name to 400 pages.
she goes to the Park and Recreations Dept.
where they're rehearsing *Cabaret*.
they almost give her a part as a whore
but they really need an older
whore.

when she comes back
we go out for a drive.
I bite her on the left ear
in my publisher's rose garden.
this is to give her fair warning
that greater obligations
might soon arrive.

her millionaire is
retired, wears bedroom slippers, smokes
continually. when she mentions my name
or one of my books, he
nods: "ah, yes, Chinaski."
he is a stamp collector and a
gentleman to the
last. we share
her. he
with his money and I
with my poems.

we drive about in her red
Porsche. she drives
well
with irritation but also with a
general
maturity.

the lady before her drove as if she could not
see past the windshield wipers;
besides that
she began fucking nearly
everybody.
I felt that
was a direct insult to my love-making
if not my
poetry.

this one
likes scotch
radio up good and loud
burning cigarettes left
everywhere.

a flame
rises
the couch is on
fire
I put it out with
tall glasses of
water.

when we go to bed she
lights a
candle.
Shostakovitch screams from the
radio, we
kiss and fondle.
ears
tongues
hair
feet
breathing.

we fuck. we fuck and fuck and
fuck.

piers catch on fire
fall into water off
Long Island

the red-winged wallow-tail flies
north
the porch-billed ginny-bird flies
south

"spray me! spray me!" she says.
mush and raisins, red onion
slices: I blow it all
in.

washrag
she brings me a
washrag.

I wipe off
toss the rag against the
ceiling. we've done
it.

resting against the headboard we
drink scotch
watch the candle
feel good
then alternately feel
bad
because there's so much living
behind us;
shamed, in a sense, because we're old dogs
trying to
cross the street against the
signal. we smoke

too many
cigarettes.

the night gets
us.

we weary.

I am wrapped around the back of
her
close and soothing;
she snores but not too
loudly;
I feel her hair in my
nostrils.

sounds come from outside:
sirens
stupefied drunks
beggars
serial murderers.
she's like a
child, must be careful,
you just got away from a bad one, a real
bad one: she chewed you up and
spit you out like a
piece of
gum.

the land drops away
the ocean puts out the candle
I finally sleep.

take the grace
take the luck
take the apples without the worms.

candles? what do candles
mean?

even Shakespeare got
burned by one of
them.

THE BIG LONELY NIGHT

Helen, where are we?
who stole the licorice?
where's Grandfather's clock?
not even a mouse around.
devil take it, where's my pipe?
is the door locked?
it's a world full of stranglers,
bad food, dense attitudes,
drunken airline pilots
and ocean liners full of
opium eaters.
I need a haircut,
wonder what happened to
Blaze O'Brien the one-eyed
dentist?
if I open the closet door there'll
be a severed head in
there.
bet on it.
Helen! Helen! where are you?
damned woman, probably down-
stairs making pots of fudge.
you ever try to catch a greased pig?
I've got one foot smaller than the
other, you ever heard of that?

I haven't left this room
for three days.
I'm going to explode!
serves her right, the bitch.
HELEN!
married that woman so that she
could make fudge.
I think something's coming through
the window!
what is it?
it's smiling without a mouth.
it moves without legs.
o.k., sit down, we'll talk.
you want some fudge?
stop it!
don't turn out the light!
I'll sic my dog on you!
you bastard, I want my pipe!
Helen, get this thing off me!
HELEN!
can you hear me?
HELEN!

PART THREE

we are all
museums of fear.

ONE A.M.

cutting my toenails at
one a.m.
caught
in a tiny corner
while listening to
Tchaikovsky.

Tchaikovsky and I
always seem to
feel crappy
at the same
times (although he
is much better at
expressing
it).

I manage to
smile as I
clip off
a sliver of
nail
from the large
right
toe.

at least I'm
not yet
cutting my
throat!

just think, sweet
jesus, we are given
all these chances
to

consider and to
reconsider

while cutting our
toenails at
one a.m.

while listening to
Tchaikovsky
pathetically
wailing
in the
dark.

THE CURSE

you think that fame hasn't eaten
people alive?
hasn't killed them long before
their time?
it made Tolstoy fearful of
his wife and God;
caused Henry Miller to stop
writing books
and turn instead to
tirelessly writing love letters
to women who only wanted
to fuck
his addled
notoriety;
led poor Hemingway
down the lonely path
of electroshock treatment
and suicide;

compelled Céline, he of the
darkest laughter of our time,
to walk off into the woods
tired and broken;
hounded Ezra Pound and
Hamsun relentlessly like wild
dogs;
tricked Ambrose Bierce into
disappearing forever;
forced van Gogh to swim and drown
in a gorgeous yellow sun of his
own making;
and drove so many others to
falter and fail
all so unsuspecting
all so humanly
fragile.

we are hardly ever
as strong
as that which we
create.

WITH HIS AWFUL TEETH

this dog Sadness is gnawing at me
again.
I sit in this room with a big hole
chewed in my
side.
all I want are some gentle
moments
to fall like soft
raindrops.
they will not arrive.

this dog Sadness is a persistent
mongrel.
he finds me so often
these days,
again and again.
he is here with me now.
"go on," he growls, "write your
poem about me,
it won't make me go
away."
he's right.
I stop and look at my
wristwatch,
follow the second
hand around
and around.
it leads me nowhere.
I am trapped here with this Sad
dog.
I make small movements,
light a cigarette,
rattle a box of
paper clips.
nothing changes.
this dog of Sadness
continues to
sit here with
me,
feeding greedily.
he is getting quite
fat.
you want a pet,
my friend?
I'll give him to you right

now
along with this
poem!
if only
you would
be kind enough to
take him away,
this
Sad
dog.

GOLDEN BOY

he was six-feet-two with golden blond hair
tall
blue-eyed
a perfect muscular body
he was quiet and drove a bright yellow sports car
to school
he wore beautiful sweaters
he didn't smoke he didn't go with girls
he didn't go with boys
I'd pull up on my bicycle
put my foot on the running board and
say, "hey, Dale, why don't you go out for
football? you'd average
eight yards a carry!"
he'd tell me or anybody else:
"nonsense, I could possibly get injured
in a meaningless game."

in school we never got to him either in one way or
the other.
he stood apart.

(but they got to our principal just before we
graduated, they got him for embezzling
funds.)

in our yearbook of 1938, Winter graduating
class, Dale Thorpe's photo was in there
along with the rest of our photos
but he looked different than we did.
more poised, more confident,
completely certain of his destiny.
under each photo there was a caption about
the student:

"Likes Ping-Pong and running in
marathons."

"Engaged to a law student at U.S.C."

"Ann-Jean says she just wants to be a
housewife and mother."

"Seeks the Voice of the Turtle. An excellent
mechanical draftsman."

under Dale Thorpe's photo it said:
"Going to Paris to study painting."

Dale Thorpe of L.A. High
Winter class, 1938
what happened to him?
I waited for years in vain to know.
maybe he changed his name?
he looked so confident
so certain to succeed
with his golden blond hair
his sure sense of purpose and
that bright yellow
sports car.

SURREAL TANGERINES

will you show me how to kick this engine over
in this endless glazing rain?
it won't start.

send me the address of Hitler's burial mound.
tell me where the good whore lives.

tell me why my elbows don't drop off,
why my head doesn't roll under the bed.

don't tell me about Jesus or the devil
or about a new healthy diet.

I just want young girls to watch and wet their panties
while I kill flys with a rolled-up
newspaper.

please show me how to kick this engine over
and tell me that death is only a dream or
a bad joke.

tell me that my real desire is only for
life itself.

tell me how to get out and also stay in.

tell me how to move up and then down.

give me one more chance
one free bottle of good French wine and

a Band-Aid that will truly cover the wound.
help me kick this engine over!
give me a 15-year-old girl to
bring me a plate of tangerines
as the City of Angels goes up in flames.

let me know that my birth and your birth is more than
meaningless mathematics.

let me eat the girl
let me eat the tangerines
in that order.

it has simply rained too hard for
too
long.

please help me kick this god-damn
engine
over
one more time.

LITTLE MAGAZINES AND POETRY CHAPBOOKS

the mailman keeps bringing me more
and more little
magazines and poetry chapbooks.
as the cops bust the whores
as the terrorists hold hostages
as the wetbacks work the fields
as the Savings and Loan Associations
underpay pale thin girls
the mailman continues to stack them up
day after day
outside my door
as I listen to
Sibelius.

MY BUDDY

my head was masked with bandages
and I took the bus there
every day

where I sat on the hard long bench
and waited for the doctor.

each day about the same time
a man would walk in and sit on
the long hard bench with me.

this man's nose was growing strangely
upon itself.
it was very large and red and
long and lopsided.

under all my bandages I had my own
troubles.

we both had to wait on that bench many hours
each day.
the nurses were nice and joked
with us.

I didn't know what they were doing
to the man's nose
but it was getting worse
much worse
just like my own troubles.

we sat on the same bench each
day
but never spoke to one
another.

I remember that year well.
the weather was good almost

all year long
and at the end of the year suddenly
the man stopped coming

and the doctors and nurses
never spoke about him
nor did they seem to miss him
and I had to sit on the bench
for a long time yet
with other
more ordinary
people.

LAST FRIDAY NIGHT

sick on a Friday night while the discos rock, lots
of hip and leg, I'm too sick to drink,
listening to Brahms and squeezing orange
juice. when I'm too sick to drink you
know I'm sick. I didn't even buy
tomorrow's Racing Form. now there's
some Sibelius on the radio and
in the apartment house on the
corner a woman screams as a
man beats her.

there's nothing on TV. it's moments like this that
the madhouses are better understood. I've even
rolled a joint now. I found some old stuff in
the closet.

when Sibelius reached 40 he shaved off
all the hair on his head, walked
into his house and never
came out again until that

last day when they
came for him.

sick at the age of 57 I sit listening to
the music and smoking this poor joint
while I plan a comeback.

sick on a Friday night I understand very little. but I
like the lamplight and my cigar box keeps saying over
and over to me: *mentel charutos pimentel charutos*
pimentel charuto entel charutos pimentel charutos
pimen . . .

the woman screams again as the man beats
her. he calls her a whore. what is
he doing living with a whore?

OPEN HERE

flowers floating on the lake.
New Jersey dogs in thrall.
Rimbaud didn't really want it,
Henry Miller did.
do abandoned factories ever
scream at mid-
night?
I am warming up now as
bottle caps explode in my
brain.
I am giving off smoke.
I am really smoking now.
I am an Easter egg.
I am a paper clip.
life is
like a train thundering out of

the dark end of a tunnel,
full of fools,
the poet sitting quietly in the
passenger lounge reading
tomorrow's newspaper.

as the world reaches
its final foolish conclusion
I realize that
nothing has been learned,
that nothing
really
has meant anything
at
all.

A NAME IS NOTHING IF THE NAMED IS NOTHING

writing the good stuff in those early
days of madness and having it all
creep back to me in the mail.
and now being far from those early days
and now sometimes writing stuff that is
not so good
and getting it accepted
anyhow
which is the way it is when you
get half-a-reputation
and it was that way then
when I saw the writers with reputations
getting crap published
that was nowhere near as good
as my rejected stuff.

but that's just the way the world
is and was
and I see actors still acting
who can no longer act
and comedians still up there
dead on stage.
why do the audiences and the
powers-that-be persist
in tolerating
this shit?
I am astonished always at the
stupidity of Humanity but
I shouldn't be, it's always
with us.
which, after all,
keeps giving me more
and more
to write
about.

THE STUPIDEST THING I EVER DID

one day in New Orleans I was walking
along the sidewalk
and suddenly I began walking very
fast
as if I had an important
appointment.
I had nowhere to go, really, but I just
rushed along,
leaping off curbs
into the street, crossing, almost
running.

then I was seen by somebody who
knew me, a waitress, she was walking
the other way and she laughed and
said, "hurry! hurry!"
I waved and rushed on . . .

after a few blocks I slowed down and
went back to my normal pace
which was leisurely.
I tried to analyze why I had done what
I had done. I decided I had
wanted to be seen as someone with
a connection somewhere, with a need to take care
of something urgent.
I wanted neither, of course, I was a drifter, a bum,
an alky,
but for that moment I had weakened, I had
felt the need to be recognized as one of
them.
my brain, my spirit had failed me and
I had become a traitor to
myself.

I saw the waitress a couple of days
later at her café.
"you were in a big hurry the other
day," she smiled.

"yeah," I answered, "I had a little
something to take care of . . ."

what could I tell her?
that I had temporarily lost my mind?

I figured the town was finally getting
to me

and about a week later I
hopped a Greyhound to
Philly.

YOU CAN'T MAKE A LION OUT OF A BUTTERFLY

he was naturally big
and he was strong
he was just born that way
with curls that fell
over his forehead
he even had an English accent
and he was pretty if you
didn't look too close
all he lacked was soul and
fire.
he'd never been hungry
he'd never been lonely
he'd never been anything
but big and strong
with oversize curls
and we worked him up the
heavyweight ladder
against misfits with glass
chins.
he was 26-and-0
when we put him in against the
5th ranked contender
a black butterball
who'd been in prison three times
once for rape
once for burglary

and once for nothing at all
and our boy Bobby
looked good in
the first round
he had an 8-inch reach on Butterball
he had youth
size
strength
was perfectly trained
but Butterball came out in the 2nd
and started landing shots from the
outfield.
our boy covered up like a girl
backed against the ropes
hid under his arms
and in the 3rd it was the same
and in the 4th Butterball
got to his
chin
and
our boy Bobby fell down
took the count of 10
and got up promptly
at 11.

none of us would talk to him
in the dressing room.
he sat on the edge of the table
and said, "I'm going to take up
acting."

in the ring
right after the fight
Butterball had told me:
"that guy couldn't raise half a

hard-on in a high-class
whorehouse."

"go take your shower, Bobby,"
somebody in the room
said.

after he walked into the shower
room we looked at each
other, there were 3 or
4 of us.
now we all had to find new
jobs.

"well, no shit," somebody said.
and that's just what it really
was all
about.

I DON'T KNOW ABOUT YOU BUT

when I had rats in my room then there were
no mice
and when I had mice then there were no
roaches
and no matter where I lived
(with one exception)
all the other rooms seemed to have
decent working people living in them
and they were very quiet and polite.
too often I was the only madman
there,
behind in my rent,
depressed and alone,
wondering how I got
to where I was.

I figured it was my father's
fault,
it sure as hell couldn't be mine,
as those landladies terrorized me,
bumping their vacuum cleaners
against my door as I lay sweating
on the bed.
once in a while I'd get out and around
and luck into a bit of
money
but then always it was back to the room again,
alone and depressed again,
the shades down,
hiding out like some mole-like
creature.

at times I would visit the
neighborhood bars
and sometimes this meant
women
and it was always better with
a woman,
you could share your dismay for
the universe with
her
and when there was no food
and little hope
you could always make love again,
you had nothing but opportunity and
time.

best, of course, was striking it rich
and really getting high:
then you could pace
the floor, smoking, strutting,

telling her what a tough guy you
were, what a great man you would
become.
but those ladies were hardly
dependable:
even after she had declared her
love for you,
you'd come back to find
her gone and your little
stash gone
and then it was either
go to the bars, find her,
terrorize her and everybody else
in the bar,
or just forget it.
you planned some elaborate suicides in those
rooms,
tried a few, couldn't make any of them
work.

still, all in all, despite the fear
and madness and not
knowing how it all would end,
I loved those rooms, the
door closed, myself alone on the
bed looking at the ceiling
letting the hours and the days
and the weeks roll
by.
I memorized everything in sight:
the knobs on the dresser,
the cracks in the mirror,
the tiles in the dirty bathroom floor,
the week-old
newspaper lying on the

floor (it comforted me
to read the same headline
over and over again).
convinced it was my father's
fault, since he had told me that
I would surely be a bum,
I waited in those rooms,
waited for what seemed a lifetime
to find the answer,
a troubled young man of extreme
leisure,
and I don't know about
you
but I think somehow it was the
best time of my
life.

IT'S A DRAG JUST BREATHING

I just want a hot cup of coffee, black,
and I don't want to hear about your
troubles.
see this stump here?
I lost that hand when I jammed it
up an elephant's hot ass.
you got a sister?
can she cook?
can she work the wand?
I get a relief check every month, *I* don't
sleep in some cardboard box.
I like to watch old James Cagney
movies
but I saw something else on TV last

night, pretty good.
this guy ran around biting off people's
ears and eating them
with a touch of Tabasco sauce.
well, to each their own but you know
what really pisses me?
these ballplayers, man, getting
millions a year.
and for what? stealing 6 bases, hitting
.271 with ten homers?
give me another fucking coffee.
took my car in the other day, it was
running a little choppy.
when I came back they'd waxed it
and added a set of whitewalls.
they handed me the bill:
$857.62!
what the hell's this? I screamed,
what's the fucking 62 cents for?
the guy just shrugged his shoulders.
funny thing happened to that place. last
night it burned down to the ground.

I said I wanted another coffee!
you got shit in your ears, buddy?
another thing
I won't go to the post office anymore.
(I got a p.o. box there where women send me
nude photos of themselves along with their love
letters.)
anyhow, I try to walk in and there
are bums everywhere,
got the old hand out.
gave a guy a buck the other day while
I was going in and coming out he's

got his hand out again.
don't you remember me? I asked.
I just gave you a buck?
well, gimme another one!
he demanded.
why, you turd-sucking jackoff! I
screamed, got him in a hammer
lock and then slapped him along
side the head with my stump, made
him give me my buck back plus two
more for good luck.

why didn't you fill this cup up?
you think I'm nuts or what?
I'm not coming back to this god-damned
place if you treat me like this!
get me the manager!
what?
YOU'RE THE MANAGER?
haha, ha, ha ha!
that's the best laugh I've had in years!
damn, I feel good now!
you oughta be a comic!
one of those stand-up guys!
you'd kill 'em!
you've made me feel so good,
laughing.
I'm gonna reward you,
I'm gonna pour this hot cup of
coffee right down inside the front
of your shirt!
look!
hey, where the hell you going?
come back here, I ain't ordered my
fucking meal yet!

A HARD LESSON

the bullies of grammar school never made it past the
first turn
and most of the beautiful little girls became not so
beautiful
and he
the coward
the stammerer
the freak
finally grew tall and powerful
and only then did he
give up and
become a crank a
fidget
a loner
a drunk.
for this, they made him pay
and he paid,
gladly,
as even the mountains seemed
obscene,
as even the books of learning became
indecent.
God was not only dead but
so were all his
children.

then one day
the coward
the stammerer
the freak
went back to grammar
school again
and the seats were

empty and the teacher
was gone
and he got up and took
a piece of chalk and
wrote upon the
blackboard:

NOBODY WILL EVER SEE
THIS.

then he sat back down
satisfied
and stared at the
words.

A CONVERSATION TO REMEMBER

try shoveling sand, seems like there's nothing heavier
than sand.
what? I asked.
try shoveling sand, he said.
shut up, I said.
wanna fight? he asked.
I'll rip your god-damned head off, I told him.
maybe we better not fight then, he said.
I know you got problems, Eddie, but everybody's got
them.
wrong, Hank, some people don't have any,
they're born holding
4 aces and 3 kings.
maybe you're right, I said.
you done time? he asked.
a little, Eddie, not much.
what was the rap?

nothing much.
nobody ever admits they're guilty, Hank.
everybody's guilty, Eddie.
shut up, he said.
wanna fight? I asked.
I'll rip your god-damned head off, he told me.
maybe we better not fight then, I said.
you oughta try shoveling sand sometime, he said.
what? I asked.
sand, he said, sand.

we'd been drinking 3 or 4 hours.
it was a night late in April and the world was still
there.
it was late and April was still there waiting
in the night and we'd been drinking for
3 or 4 hours, maybe
5.

PICTURE SHOW

it's a horror show and it's
free, cowardice is revered
as Mr. Ticket Taker
takes tickets at the door.
it's crowded as we push toward
death.
lights flash, thunder roars, clowns
smile.
the show
is on the big screen.
the only mercy is no mercy.
there are no answers, only
questions.

false laughter smears the
air.
there is nothing to forget and
nothing to
remember.
the mad and the sane are
inseparable.
the dead breed more dead.
the foul sea and the foul earth
swallow us all.
our first breath
our first day
on earth
only restarts the
horror
here.

HE PLAYED FIRST BASE

everybody on the team hated him.
he had handsome features
a perfect muscular body
arms like fence posts.
he never joked in the locker room
he just kept hitting the baseball
leading the league in batting average,
homers, doubles, triples, RBIs
and total bases.
and he got all the TV commercials
and all the girls
and he just kept on hitting that
baseball.
he was MVP in his second season in

the Majors but
even the manager disliked
him
and the next season he dropped him
from the cleanup spot to
number 5.
he got off slowly
and the whole league was delighted
but in the second half of the season
he came on again
and led the team in everything but
stolen bases.
his wife divorced him
because of the girls
and then he got some bad press
but he meant a pennant for the team
a trip to the play-offs
and possibly he'd take them
all the way to the World
Series.

he was the
all-American boy
walking out of the shower room
looking clean and fresh and wholesome.

someday he'd suffer
someday he'd feel some real pain
someday the women would have his balls
someday he'd have to become
human.

nobody could keep on getting away
with that kind of shit
forever.

THE SUICIDE KID

I went to the worst of bars
hoping to get
killed.
but all I could do was to
get drunk
again.
worse, the bar patrons even
ended up
liking me.
there I was trying to get
pushed over the dark
edge
and I ended up with
free drinks
while somewhere else
some poor
son-of-a-bitch was in a hospital
bed,
tubes sticking out all over
him
as he fought like hell
to live.
nobody would help me
die as
the drinks kept
coming,
as the next day
waited for me
with its steel clamps,
its stinking
anonymity,
its incogitant

attitude.
death doesn't always
come running
when you call
it,
not even if you
call it
from a shining
castle
or from an ocean liner
or from the best bar
on earth (or the
worst).
such impertinence
only makes the gods
hesitate and
delay.
ask me: I'm
72.

SNAKE EYES AND FAULTY SCREAMS

you tell me where it's at, Lincoln. I've got sun spots before
my
eyes, I'm wearing this rubber band around my left
wrist, the troops have come marching home, they've
closed down the Mermaid's Lament, Tilly's got the blues,
Pruit has moved back in with his mother, the circus is
down at Ports O'Call and Randy Jack sits in the halfway
house
working crossword puzzles.
Lincoln, tell me where it's at when the fuzz comes off the
peach and the monkey steals from the accordion man.

I don't expect an eternal shining light but they've sat us
down
in this pukey dark and left us diddling with broken
dreams.
grandma told me to look them in the eye and to shoot
from the hip
but when I did
they did.
once more,
I'll bet you George Washington's wooden teeth against the
Katzenjammer Kids that you can't tell a Tabanus
from a Hemichordate!
they've called off the dogs but have you seen the YoYo
Man?
the power is on but are the lines cut?
is what's good for the goose sometimes only good for the
goose?
meanwhile, Lincoln, your time is up and my time is down
and there is something in the back room moving
tongueless, eyeless, legless,
more magnificent than glass,
impartial as the toothpick
as *snap* go the strings of my heart.

I FOUGHT THEM FROM THE MOMENT I SAW LIGHT

I, for one, was willing to fight
for soul or grail or banner.
I mounted a machine gun
in the center of my room
and though I was 4-f and damn glad of it
I have seen plenty of war pictures

(that's the best way to do it).
I surrounded myself with cold beer,
with the memories of warm women
and also with some good symphonies I had heard
back during the time
when I had the guts to climb mountains
(but my beard is gray now
and I cackle through broken teeth
like an old hen with a worm).

the phone has now rung several times, a
shower of meaningless sound,
and my boss asks, "where the hell
are you? what's happening? when are you
coming in?"

I put the phone down like the handle of a hot frying pan,
re-check my ammo belt and stare north at the
purple mountains
over Hollywood, estimating their distance in metric feet
and wondering if I might be buried near them
if anybody bothers to bury me at all?

"it is understood," says another voice on the phone,
"that under the terms of the divorce,
if you fail to make the payments on the car,
the car goes to me."

"I've always failed to make payments on everything
because everything has always failed to make payments
to me," I reply.

but I think I must be a happy man and
this makes for poetry and pain and confusion
and a 4-f kind of life
because a man is pretty damn well out-gunned
from day one.

but as I re-check my ammo belt there is a knock
upon the door: "rent's due! cough up,
you bastard!"

I touch the trigger lightly, quite lightly
like Chopin at the piano
and spin a lovely pattern in the wood—
through the holes I can see moths and blackbirds
dying in the hall
and the voice stops.

now I can hear sirens, and people,
people are gathering outside in the street; well,
I have plenty of good bullets left and a record player
and I hear if you piss in a hanky it's as good as
a gas mask. I only hope you read this sooner rather than
later
because if you read it later
in the *Times* or *Mirror* or *Examiner*
I'll be dead, and I was just beginning to write some
real good poetry—
    and now I think
        maybe I should have
learned to pray, because the preacher will say
(they always crap on the newly fallen) that
I got what was coming to me,
but he'd better stay out of the way now
or get a gut-full too.

I'm Chopin, drunk, clutching my Polack soul,
the last bad man,
while all around me
the whores are selling their bodies
like beautiful things
like beautiful things that bloom.

NOW, EZRA,

you more than anybody, knew what the
poem is! a trick, a toy, to be worked on
at whim to fit fanciful patterns.
work it well enough and
then profound or
seemingly profound meanings surface
on the page.
but, essentially, it was just shuck and jive
for you
just as it is for everybody
else.
there was/is nothing holy to say.
there never will be anything holy to say.
we live, we die, right?
and are each caught, in between
this way and that way.
it's pure folly to get slick about
all this.
we all come up short in the
end.
the worst say it badly.
the luckiest say it a bit differently,
bored with what has preceded them,
they just say nothing in a newer
way,
to hold that ground for a decade or
two,
(or a century or two)
in order to be
safely preserved in textbook
minds—

hardly a reward
for the simple hell of every
day living.

yes, poetry is a lie.

CONCESSION

did you ever see a horse with
a broken leg
trying to stand on that
leg?
I don't have the guts to watch, I
have to look away up into the
grand-stand and there another terrible
sight awaits me, all those human faces
and I have to look away again as
the darkness descends and you
become aware of your heart, your
throat, your despair, your mind and
what's left of your spirit, that's
when the death-wish arrives, that's
when you know that you've never
accomplished anything worthwhile—so
cart the horse away, nuke the humans
and the cities, trash history,
just leave standing there my shoes, untied,
the left one upright, the right one on
its side, there like that, frozen
in time, empty forever.

IT

if it doesn't get you now
it surely will get you later
and before it gets you later
it's going to take some others now
so there won't be so many to take
later.

it's been busy everywhere you know,
public and private.
sometimes it happens almost overnight,
other times it takes a bit longer
but it never misses,
the sweep is clean.

bathing beauties turn into scrub ladies,
orators spit out their vocal cords,
great hitters go blind at the plate,
tightrope walkers tremble in space,
invincible heavyweights crumble to the canvas,
the world's greatest painter takes his shotgun into the
cornfields,
funeral follows funeral in caterpillar hush,
it's all so sad, really so sad, I just can't talk about it
any
more.

TERROR

the terror is viewing the human
face
and then hearing it talk
and watching the creature
move.
the terror is knowing its
motives.
the terror is seeing it
skinned,
opened
for an internal view of its
spirit.
the terror is looking into its
eyes.
the terror is knowing the
centuries of its
doings.
the terror is the unchangeability
of it.
its multiplicity,
its duplicity is
terrifying.
it's everywhere, this giant mass
of Humanity
self-revered,
self-serving,
self-destructive,
the terror of no selves
spreading from here into
space,
cluttering the universe,
marring pure open space,

poisoning hope,
raping chance,
going on,
this massive zero of
non-life
labeled
Humanity,
the terror, the
horror,
the waste of it and
you and
me
through and
through and
through.

MY ROSY ASS

I'm naturally right-handed but
Kirby wants me to be a switch-hitter again.
I showed him the figures:
as a right-hander last season I hit
.301 against all comers and
batting left I made nothing but outs.
"doesn't matter," he said, leaning
back in his office chair,
"I want you to switch-hit."
"the figures don't support you,
Kirby, you're just going by your own
book."
"I'm managing this fucking team
and there's a good reason for that,"
he said.

"you're gonna be a
switch-hitter."
"fuck you, man, I'll hit the way
I want!"
"you won't be in the lineup,
then!"
"Kirby, I'm getting $900,000
this season and if you want me
to sit on my rosy ass, that's
up to you."
"the conversation is over,"
Kirby said. "get the hell out of
here!"
I walked around behind his
desk.
"you son-of-a-bitch, I got a
good mind to kick your
butt!"
"my hands are flat on the
desk, you touch me and you're
gone!"
I thought about it, then turned
around, slammed the door and
was out of there.

I went down to the parking lot, got in
my car and headed
home.

it was a hot, stupid drive
featuring a 3 car pile-up on the
freeway.

as I pulled up the drive
my wife and her mother were
standing in the garden.

they waved and smiled.
what the hell did they know?
I should have kicked Kirby's
butt.
I drove into the garage and
hit the lawn mower and a garbage can.
it made a terrible noise.
in the rear view mirror I see my
wife and her mother
approaching.
they are going to ask me
what happened.
and I am going to tell them
I hit the fucking lawn mower
and the fucking garbage can,
that's what
happened!

THIS IS A BITTER POEM

are my writer friends
all about the
same?

I would have to think that they
are.

for example
sometimes one or another
of them is in
trouble
and
sometimes

I help
out.

and
usually
what I do
helps them escape
(at least, for a
time)
whatever crisis
they were
in.

and then I
forget about
that
and
go about doing
other
things.
but they
remember
and reward
me

usually with a
copy of their
book-length
manuscript—

a novel or a sheaf of
poesy—

informing me
that
they have
used my name

without permission and
submitted the
manuscript
to my
editor-
publisher.

then they sit back
and
wait
for me to speak up
on their behalf
leaving the guilt
and shame
for me to deal
with as best
I can.

POEM FOR NOBODY

an apprehension for reality, the death of the flower,
the collapse of hope, the crush of
wasted years, the nightmare faces,
the mad armies attacking for no reason at all
and/or
old shoes abandoned in old corners like half-forgotten
voices that once said love but did not mean
love.

see the face in the mirror? the mirror in the
wall? the wall in the house? the house in the
street?

now always the wrong voice on the telephone
and/or

the hungry mouse with beautiful eyes which now lives in
your brain.

the angry, the empty, the lonely, the
tricked.

we are all
museums of fear.

there are
as many killers as flies as
we dream of giant
sea turtles with strange words carved into
their hard backs
and no place for the knife to go in.
Cain was Able,
ask him.
give us this day our daily dread.

the only solace left to us is to hide
alone in the middle of night in some deserted
place.

with each morning less than zero,
humanity is a hammer to the brain,
our lives a bouquet of blood, you can watch
this fool still with his harmonica
playing elegiac tunes while
slouching toward Nirvana
without
expectation or
grace.

CHECKMATE

we are broken down bit by bit,
we
drain away by the minute, the hour, the week, the
month, the year, we
leak away
in cafés, backyards, stadiums, parking lots, in
parlors of chance, in movie houses, at church,
at clambakes,
we dissolve
we dissolve while
putting on our shoes, while
putting out the cat, while
turning out the light,
while clipping our toenails.
so we continually dissolve from substance to
shadow, endlessly
dissolve while listening
to bad music or in total silence,
forever dissolve
while reading old love letters and new books,
during peace and war,
on and off TV.
thus our lives dissolve and disappear between the helmet
and
a high-heeled shoe, between an olive seed and a buried
corpse, between a lost key and the exposed film, between
a
child's smile and the magnolia's scream.

THE TIDE

ten minutes before post time
the horses, jocks, outriders
arrive
for the post parade.
most of the people go to
watch.

usually about six minutes to
post
the parade is over
and here they come:
THE TIDE.

they come sweeping in
to the betting windows:
little bent women
cheap hold-up men
the unemployed
the intoxicated
the crippled
the mad
the damned
the dull
the bored
the dull and the bored
the worn
the gimpy
the shameless
the defeated and the driven
the child molesters
the pickpockets
the Food Stampers
the muggers

the wetbacks
the clerk typists
the wife-beaters
your friends and
mine.

THE TIDE comes
sweeping in
to the betting windows:
they *know* something.
they're ready.
now
is the time.

THE TIDE
arrives
all at once.

the lines jam
up.

people leap from
line to line.

"why don't they
open more windows?"

there they stand,
waiting.

and as the time
gets down to the
last minute or two
desperation overtakes
many
who feel they won't
have time to
get their bets down.

voices are heard:
"HEY, COME ON! COME ON!
MOVE IT!"

then the announcer is heard
over the loudspeaker:
*"the horses are approaching
the gate!"*

the voices get more urgent,
louder: "COME ON! COME ON!
MOVE IT!"

now
at this last moment
there appears to be just one
kind of bettor:
the sadist.

the sadists are very
good:
they time it so that
they arrive
at the betting window
with almost no time
left.
yes, the sadists
do prefer to
place their bets in time
but they are *more*
interested
in torturing
the people waiting
behind them.

*"the horses are now
at the gate!"* the

announcer is heard over
the speakers.

the sadists now
use all manner of ploys
to keep the other people
from placing their bets.

most of the sadists
lean right through
the betting window
drop their bellies
against the wood
get comfortable
and *slowly*
begin to make their
tiny little
bets:
"ah, let's see now . . .
ummm . . . 2 dollars to show
on the 9 . . . and let's
see . . . I think I'll have
$2 to place on the 6 . . . no,
hold it . . . make it $2 to place
on the 9 . . . wait, what race
is this? . . . is this the 2nd
race? . . . oh, it's the first?
listen, could you cancel
those tickets? o.k., now
give me $2 to win on the 4.
is this an exacta race?"

the sadists also converse loudly
with the teller.
any conversation at all

will do: "did Shoemaker
scratch off of the 8 horse?"

then
finally
after making their miserable
bets
they don't have their
money ready.

and often they drop
their program
have to bend down
and look for it.

they don't have their
money ready,
ever.
if it's a man
he starts to fumble in his
pockets
for it.

if it's a woman
she plops
a huge purse
on the counter
slowly opens it
and begins
to search
inside.

sometimes it's hard
to tell
the sadists from the
stupid people who
wait behind them.

finally it's certain
that a portion of
THE TIDE
is going to be
shut out
from placing their
bets.

"HOLY SHIT!" somebody
screams, "I'VE GOT THE
WINNER AND I CAN'T
BET!"

but the strange part of
this tale
is that
all the smart money
has been wagered
before THE TIDE
came rushing in:
the midgets
the whores
the unemployed air-controllers
the displaced auto workers
the fortune-tellers
the glass-blowers
the night watchmen
the female-libbers
the dog catchers on sick leave
members of the city council
private dicks
bank examiners
bit men
hit men
your friends and
mine.

I repeat:
all the smart money
is in
just before
THE TIDE
came rushing in
and if you can separate
what the public thinks from
reality
that's all you
need to know to bet
wisely.

I now bet with 7 minutes to
go
when getting into line
doesn't seem
like a victory at
all
but it
is.

thus I
no longer deal
with THE TIDE.

most of what we learn
in this crazy life is
what to
avoid.

like, say,
a fancy ending
to this poem.

TO HELL AND BACK

they say that
hell is crowded yet
when you're in hell
you always seem to be
alone.

and you can't tell
anyone when
you are in hell
or they'll think
you're
crazy.

and being crazy is
being in hell
and being sane is hellish
too.

those who escape hell
however
never talk about
it
and nothing much
bothers them
after
that.
I mean, things like
missing a meal,
going to jail,
wrecking your car
or
even
the idea of

death
itself.

when you ask them,
"how are things?"
they'll always answer, "fine,
just fine . . ."

once you've been to hell
and back,
that's enough, it's the
greatest satisfaction
known to man.

once you've been to hell
and back,
you don't look behind you
when the floor
creaks and
the sun is always up at
midnight
and things like
the eyes of mice
or an abandoned tire
in a vacant lot
can make you
smile

once you've been to hell
and back.

SOMETHING'S KNOCKING AT THE DOOR

a great white light dawns across the
continent
as we fawn over our failed traditions,
often kill to preserve them
or sometimes kill just to kill.
it doesn't seem to matter: the answers dangle just
out of reach,
out of hand, out of mind.

the leaders of the past were insufficient,
the leaders of the present are unprepared.
we curl up tightly in our beds at night and wait.
it is a waiting without hope, more like
a prayer for unmerited grace.

it all looks more and more like the same old
movie.
the actors are different but the plot's the same:
senseless.

we should have known, watching our fathers.
we should have known, watching our mothers.
they did not know, they too were not prepared to
teach.
we were too naive to ignore their
counsel
and now we have embraced their
ignorance as our
own.
we are them, multiplied.
we are their unpaid debts.
we are bankrupt
in money and
in spirit.

there are a few exceptions, of course,
but these teeter on the
edge
and will
at any moment
tumble down to join the rest
of us,
the raving, the battered, the blind and the sadly
corrupt.

a great white light dawns across the
continent,
the flowers open blindly in the stinking wind,
as grotesque and ultimately
unlivable
our 21st century
struggles to be
born.

REGARDLESS

the nights you fight best
are
when all the weapons are pointed
at you,
when all the voices
hurl their insults
while the dream is being
strangled.

the nights you fight best
are
when reason gets
kicked in the
gut,

when the chariots of
gloom
encircle
you.

the nights you fight best
are
when the laughter of fools
fills the
air,
when the kiss of death is
mistaken for
love.

the nights you fight best
are
when the game is
fixed,
when the crowd screams
for your
blood.

the nights you fight best
are
on a night like
this
as you chase a thousand
dark rats from
your brain,
as you rise up against the
impossible,
as you become a brother
to the tender sister
of joy and

move on

regardless.

PART FOUR

blue marigolds grow
in this abandoned graveyard.

THE DANDY

the famous "Hollywood" sign up on the mountain
has been slowly falling apart
and after the recent rain
it is now much worse:
the first "o" has slipped a little
and has broken in half
and the third "o" has fallen away completely
so now the sign reads:
"H_ullywo d."
I stopped in at the Gower Gulch
Shopping Center
for a new pair of prescription
sunglasses
and as I parked
I saw this man pushing a
shopping cart filled with
bottles, pieces of cloth, newspapers,
magazines, wire and bits and pieces of
nameless debris.
but each hair
on the man's head was
artistically combed and was a lovely
majestic gray.
he had a firm square chin
bright blue eyes
a new scarf around his neck
and decent clean clothes
as he *strolled* with his cart
poised and confident
puffing on a pipe
looking natty and serene and
intelligent

in fact
he looked a hell of a lot
better than I
did
(and maybe better than
you do)
this shopping cart bum
there in Gower Gulch
on Sunset Boulevard
just east of the
Mark C. Bloome
Tire Co.
at 11:45 a.m.
in
H_ullywo d.

I AM A MOLE

Chinaski only lets movie stars visit him
now, a poet wrote recently,
and while it's true that I might not have been
eager for a visit from *him*
I have also turned down requests for visits from
many others (famous and infamous)
in the entertainment business
including one of its best known rock
stars.
it's also true that none of them wanted to
visit me *before* I garnered my minor
fame.

I was *always* a loner:
if I had a telephone it was usually left off the
hook

and
people who knocked at my door seldom were
acknowledged.

now because I haven't changed my nature
this poet thinks that I am a
snob.

in the good old days people just assumed that I
was crazy. life was simple then.

all I need now is what I needed then: a desk lamp,
the typer, the bottle, the radio, classical
music, and this room
on fire.

SOMEBODY ELSE

a hangover at 70
can seem worse,
of course,
than one at
35,
but as far as
most other things
are concerned
I am the same man
now:
my strengths, my
ideals, my
confusions,
my fears,
all remain as
before.

it is only when
say
I am walking
along
and I see my
reflection
in a
plate glass
window
that I wonder,
what is
that?

that thing
there?

who is
that ugly
old man?

he frightens me.

IBM SELECTRIC

humming,
it will do almost anything you
ask it to do.

humming
beneath its smooth gray paint

*the machine
knows.*

even death stands back and
asks, "what the hell is
this?"

humming,
it astonishes the walls, the
windows, the cats, the ashtray,
the wooden Buddha and
me.

this machine can save my life.

this machine *has* saved my
life.

this machine can create a woman
more beautiful than
any you have ever seen
or
it can
punch a bully in the
nose.

humming,
this machine is
love found again
in a flood of
fire.

this machine is
a dance floor
a wild circus
a refuge for the
nearly insane.

this machine
sprouts tiny flowers of courage
in the middle of the
night.

this machine
throws off sparks of light

when the dark is as dark as
dark can get.

when I recognize
the futility of my
efforts,
when I feel
age like the blade of death,
when I feel
like jumping out of the window
at 2 a.m.
this machine
this amazing machine
stands between me
and that

as it creates
magical poems on
8 ½ by 11
sheets of paper
which
literally save
my poor
ass.

this old electric
typewriter
that sounds like
a
washing
machine.

WHY OH WHY AND OH WHY NOT?

as I back my $35,000 car
down the driveway of my paid-for home, I wonder what
happened
to the errand boy, the sleeper in parks, the beggar of
drinks, the failed suicide, the rejected young writer, the
ugly lover of ugly women, the certified failure, the pitied
clown.
I back out and now I'm on the street and I punch the
radio, luck
on to Brahms, gun around a slow driver and then I am on
the
freeway.

it happened slow and it happened fast: from idiot to
successful idiot.

then I smile.
hell, I was only giving myself time, taking
notes, gladly hosting
the horrors and the hells and the madwomen, it all was
not entirely
without humor and guile
even those nights of
sweating on the bed, actually gripping the headboard
with my hands
for fear of walking into the kitchen where
in that battered drawer
huddled the
bread knife.

it had all been part of a plan and it had all not been part
of a plan.

I take the fast lane on the freeway, the powerful motor

silent as
Brahms dances about the interior, I am alone and
astonished,
pay over $20,000 in quarterly tax and still manage to
write some of the best poetry
of our time.

MOVIES

by continuing to attend we make many of those
producers, directors and actors
very rich.
they make millions of dollars, marry one another,
live in mansions, and once a year at the Academy Awards
they heap praise upon
themselves. all this causes them to believe that
they have actually done something important but
it's only the mind-less public which watches and
swallows their tasteless pap, which makes
them rich, which turns some of them into so-
called legends, which then exaggerates their pitiful
talent.

fools turn other fools into idols.

the people waste their lives and their minds
sitting in the dark

as more and more movies are made.

NO LUCK AT ALL

at ten a.m.
behind the bar where the
beer trucks unloaded
I stretched out in the alley
and waited
there where the trucks passed
through;
but the black children
who lived in the shacks
back there
didn't understand
and I was saved by little
black girls and boys
6 and 7 years old
who waved and screamed the
beer truck down.
I only got a lot of
dirt on my clothing
and the truck driver picked
me up: "hey! you again?
asshole! don't you know
I got a schedule?"

I went back to my room
#302
and I closed all the
windows
stuffed the bottom of the door
with rags and newspapers
then turned on the
gas heater
the oven and

all the burners on the stove
without lighting them.

I stretched out on the bed
and listened to the hissing
sounds
it was almost humorous
and peaceful:
"*hissssssss!*"
from the many vents
working together.

I lost consciousness.

then I shot up in bed
sitting straight up from the
hips
I sat there
with a headache like I had
never had before
it felt as if there was a
steel band locked about my
forehead
or worse.

I got up and opened the
windows and ran about
turning off all the unlit
vents.

then I went out for
two six-packs of beer.

as I got out of the elevator
coming back
the old woman in #305
opened her door and
asked me as I put the key

into my door:
"do you smell gas?"
and I said, "no, I don't smell
gas."
and thankfully it was true:
I didn't.

GOOD NEWS

"don't worry," I tell my publisher,
"I am still in the frying pan and
the flame is turned up
high."

moving toward 72
the dangers of my becoming
complacent and
self-satisfied
are damn near
nil.
the gods have
arranged for my
journey
from beginning to
end
to be relentlessly
hellish.
it began with unbelievable
parents
and continues with
unbelievable
humanity.

you will not find me at
literary gatherings
holding a cocktail
glass.
you will not see me
on TV
as a guest on a
popular
talk show.
you probably will not see
me
at all
but if you do
I will tell you that
I have nothing to say
that I haven't already
said.

the flame is turned up high.

I have much to
celebrate.

BEDPAN NIGHTMARE

5 days a week
I find myself dueling some
son-of-a-bitch
on the freeway and
I usually
win.

death has never mattered
very much to
me.

I can well understand
how a man can
stick his head into
the mouth of a
lion
or walk through a nest of
snakes.

I am satisfied
with my aggressive nature
as I tickle death
under the
armpits.

the nightmare is not
death itself
but the half-death,
the three-quarters death, the
fractional death,
in bed in a hospital room with
strangers in charge of you
with their
bedpans,
pettiness and
bad
tempers.

and the odds are that
they will be strangers of
no-gamble,
wizened souls
with heavy dull plodding
footsteps, thick red
ankles, ugly
eyes,

wasted human beings
mumbling tired
platitudes.

better to die on the freeway of
life with
gibbering monkey-folk
surrounding your
dying ass . . .

today I scorched this
guy
on the freeway in a
late model low-slung
car,
bright red, I
hate those bright red
sons-of-bitches.
when I see red
I get like a
bull.

I wonder what he's doing
tonight?
he probably lives with his
mother and
drinks
warm milk.

ROBERT

15 minutes before noon
and no handle
anywhere;
death is a pig;
the jealous father murdered his young
son with
hot candle wax;
I know a guy who hit 50 home runs
and never listened to
Mozart once;
my car out there:
all 4 tires flat
and a 49-year-old blonde with runs
in her panty hose
vomiting in the back seat.

there's no way to go but down
there's no way to go but up
in a
day crawling with spiders.

there's a time to weep
a time to die
and a time to live.

the phone rings and a woman asks me:
"St. George Hotel?"

"no," I answer, "this is little Peter Redhut."

"is Robert there?" she asks.

you might as well try to eat a sackful of sand
as attempt to locate the bunghole of a
flamingo.

when the bellboy finally arrives
he'll show you how to differentiate between the dead
and the
living:
one brings flowers
the other ignores them;
one speaks of love
the other doesn't need it;
one sleeps
the other becomes.

dirty language comes out of a
dirty life;
commas, semicolons, question marks,
periods
abound. the phone
rings again:

"is Robert there?"
she asks.

PRIVATE SCREENINGS

the crowd at private screenings is the
worst
shaking hands with the director,
smiling joyously and telling him that
he has created a great
work
while others cluster around
waiting to tell the director that he has
created a great
work.

some of them believe it, others are
lying out of fear or
kindness.
me?
I say to my wife, "how the hell do we
get out of here?"
"you should say something to him,"
she says.
"all right," I say.
I go up to the director, pump his hand
and say,
"I liked the ending."
he smiles at me, he's excited.
then my wife and I get out of there.
sure, I liked the ending, that meant the
thing was over.

Hollywood is so self-congratulatory.
take the hundreds of films
made every year,
out of them all, there might be 4 or 5
passable ones,
maybe.

we walk out to the parking lot.
and I promise myself that the next movie
I'll *pay* for
so I can walk out without
hurting the director's
feelings.

AS YOU SLOW DOWN THE MERMAIDS LOOK THE OTHER WAY

getting out of bed each morning is hard: after all,
you've lived a long time and basically there's only
one big surprise left.

yet once you get up and into motion the past is forgotten,
everything is in the future, including the big surprise.

your wife is there, the cats are there, the automobile is
there.

once you get behind the wheel you're 16
again and
the city you've lived in since 1923 is still there for you
and you know each other well.
men and cities grow and learn to love
one another.

you drive to the racetrack, a horrible place, you've
tossed away years watching
countless thousands of horse races, you've wasted a
lifetime
there but
somehow it's a good place to hide
like the bars used to be.

you could have spent your days
going to art shows, plays, ballets, museums,
you could have spent your days painting the years away
but
you gambled on yourself instead,
still do.

and gamblers are dry and empty souls, their hearts have
been

sucked dry, there's no music in their walk, they are colorless
and condemned.
like so many others they want something for nothing and it
never works that way.

you park at the racetrack, you get out, angle toward the track entrance.
you've watched newsboys come and go, the mutuel clerks grow old,
the
jockeys get fat, the track stewards age and die,
the horses go lame and
retire.

you are the last constant on the scene, still moving toward the
action.

the clouds say hello, the sun winks and says
hello.

you walk into it all

life-worn
an old man
a dusty-shoed freak,
half-buttoned to the
universe.

looking for
something to do
between the placenta and
the big surprise

you
take the escalator
up.

SOMETHING NEW

I wonder
what am I doing in the
clubhouse?
I used to sit in the
grandstand
on the cement sun deck
and I'd see the men
I used to work with in
the factories and in the civil
service jobs.

what am I doing in the
clubhouse?

I meet the maître d'
of a famous restaurant.
we greet each other,
talk about the 3rd race
and its
possibilities.

the race goes off.

he wins
I lose.

what am I doing in the
clubhouse?

THE SWIMMING POOL

he's my photographer, he takes photos
for my books and other things.
he's a nice enough fellow but he just
doesn't understand the real
world.
lately he has been urging me to get
into the swimming pool
for a photo.
"damn it," I'll scream at him,
"are you trying to ruin my book
sales?
people will see me in the pool and
they'll know I'm a fat, stupid,
satisfied person!"
he just looks at me and his next
question is always the
same:
"well," (smiling) "then how about in the
spa?"
"no, no! no god-damned spa!"

the reading public wants a man hanging
from the cross, dying of drink, going slowly
mad, *starving.*
I may be dying of drink, going slowly mad,
but I'm not starving
and to see me photographed
complacent in a swimming pool
is going to convince them
that I am no longer able to
write.

over and over I've explained
to the photographer, "now, it's all right for

me to write about the swimming
pool if I do it in a manner
which disarms their suspicions.
or I can write about my spa
or my new car or how I won $800
at the track
today
but photographs, actual *photographs*
of me in a swimming pool or in a spa
or in or near a new car,
THIS IS DEATH!
don't you understand?"

he looks at me and
smiles.

he just doesn't understand.

THE GREAT WRITER

he thought he had developed a special
misanthropy
and had achieved a splendid
isolation from common humanity
in this latter part of his life.
then he found out otherwise
at a poetry reading tonight
when his hands shook so
badly
that he was ashamed to be
seen in
public.

another hero
gone.

I USED TO THINK

what a great experience it would have been
to sit around drinking and bullshitting
with Hemingway and Pound, e.e. cummings,
Gertrude Stein, Dos Passos, Lawrence, etc.
but when I think about the writers that I've actually met,
great and small, medium and rare,
I have second thoughts
and I realize that
the writers back then must have been just as
bitchy, just as gossip-minded, just as
self-centered,
just as dull and obnoxious in person
as those I have actually known. they too,
back in the glamorous roaring 20's,
probably began to drool after the
3rd drink, began babbling about their
literary and sexual prowess in
unbearably loud voices without the least
hint of humor.

those we elect to be our literary
idols
can be such jackasses, such assholes in
the flesh.
it's as if they have given their all to getting
the line down on paper and after that
there's simply nothing left of
them.
poor dears, drained of their
senses, they've left it all on paper
like when they wipe their butts.

I stay away from other writers, I work
alone with the door

closed
and celebrate, among other things,
their total absence,
for they *are* absent,
those chattering bitching
ninnies
who are so quick to insist
in the literary journals
and elsewhere
that I am
not one of
them.

FROM THE DEPARTMENT OF HEALTH

it's all on the right side:
bad right eye, bad right
arm, bad right
leg and
when the other side
begins to go
then I'm really in
trouble.
I always thought I'd
be able to
continue living as
always:
bulky, innocuous,
impervious
to pain.
death, of course,
would finally come,
but life would

go on as usual
until then.

now each time
the valet
at the track
opens the car door
for me
a fierce pain
shoots down through
the right leg
as I climb in.
I smile, curse,
tell the man
I'll see him
tomorrow.
I wink at him with
my good left
eye and
grind out of
there.
death is being good to
me, giving me
plenty of
warning.

at least the horses
are running
well.
I can't run from
anything
anymore.

since I never got
killed in any of my
youthful barroom brawls

now
I suppose
I'll have to go
through ordinary
channels just like
the rest of you
dogsuckers.

WORKING OUT

"are you going upstairs to write
in order to
pay your taxes?" my wife asks.
I owe the government $12,000.00
and the state $3.00
I sit down and square off in front of the
computer.
"dance, baby," I say.
it just looks back at me, a blank
blue screen.
(in the old days it was blank white
paper.)
I wait on the computer.
nothing happens.
I got to the mouse and move to a new
icon: STUPID GAMES.
I choose "Tao"
and begin to play, challenging the
computer.

my muse walks over to the
refrigerator, gets a beer, opens it,
sits down, takes a gulp and
waits.

MY FRIEND WILLIAM BURROUGHS

it was a reading in Santa Cruz.
I had a room at the Holiday Inn
and the afternoon before the reading
the young bloodsuckers knocked and came with
their six-packs of beer.
"hey," one of them said,
"guess who's in the room next to yours?"
"I dunno."
"William Burroughs," he said.
"oh?"
"don't you want to go meet him?"

we drank awhile and then I decided to take
a walk.
the young bloodsuckers followed me out
and as we passed W.B.'s place
he was sitting in a chair staring out of the
plate glass window.
I ignored him
he ignored me
and the world ignored us both.

I read the first night
he read the second.
I was unable to attend his reading
and flying back
in a good mood
with my money in my pocket
I ordered double vodka 7's all the way
in.

it was a decent flight and even the food
was good
for a change.

A NOTE UPON STARVATION

I'm not sure where I starved the worst:
Savannah, Atlanta, New Orleans, Philadelphia
or Los Angeles.
starving is not as terrible as it might
seem.
the first two or three days without
food
are the worst.
about the fourth day
you begin to feel almost intoxicated
panic subsides
one sleeps well:
12 to 14 hours,
and most unusual
one continues to defecate.
the vision grows more acute
everything is seen with a new clarity:
the stem of an apple
the tread on tires
broken glass in an alley
buttons on the shirt of a stranger
a scab on a child
dirt beneath the fingernails
street numbers painted on the curb
fireplugs just sitting there
and most of all the sun
so bright
you walk in the blazing light
and the light is everywhere
no message there
just the light
and no fear.

many unfortunate
people in the world starve to death
every day.
I think I starved worst in Atlanta.

and now
many years later
I find myself living on a fucking
diet.

POEM FOR MY 70TH BIRTHDAY

it no longer matters that the waves break on the
shore or that young girls dream and sigh.
only the next moment counts
and the next after that.

I've got to prepare myself for death: look,
there he was, now he's gone.

I think of the young man who wanted so
badly to die
and of the old man now who doesn't care whether he
does or doesn't.
the latter is best
but there is no wisdom attached.

Mahler sings for me tonight.
and this is a great cigar.
and my friend, the typewriter, sits to my left.

the dogs of night bark at something they can't
see.
they too are alert and
waiting.

YOU'LL NEVER KNOW

how come you never look directly at
anything? she asked.
how come you never look directly at
anybody? she asked.

we come in here to eat and you
don't look at the
people.
see that guy there? that's how
boys used to wear their hair
when I was a
girl.

you never look up
you never really *look* at
anything.
how are you going to learn anything
when you don't look
at anything?

we both gave our order to the
waitress and the waitress
left.

she's wearing a wig,
she told me.

after we ate we went back to her
place.

you don't have a TV, you never look at
TV, I know there's a lot of shit on TV
but you've got to *look* once in a while
or you'll never know
what's going
on.

she switched it on.

there was poor old dead Dean Martin singing with
4 young girls.

then Dean was getting his hair cut
and smoking a cigarette and the barber told
jokes and Dean told
jokes.

soon he was singing with the
4 young girls again.

you see, she said,
unless you open your eyes and
look at the world
you'll never know
what's really
out there!

JOE

this is Joe
he said
remember him?
I'm sorry
I said
I don't.

well
when we came to your last party
you were
standing in front of the fireplace
naked
and you said

208

"wait a minute you guys, I don't want you to see my
string."

I still don't remember Joe
I said.

Joe was also there
he said
when the 3 college professors came by and
you called them
3 walking sacks of
shit.

I don't remember the 3 professors
I said.

Joe
he said
was nervous because he was carrying a
needle and he didn't know the
people.

oh
I said
I see.

but Joe said he never had such a good time before.

well
I said
I see you guys brought something to
drink.

they put it
on the coffee table and I went into the
kitchen to get some
glasses. I opened the bottle and poured it
around. Benny sat on the

sofa and Joe pulled a chair
up
to the coffee table and lit a
cigarette. I noted
that he was fat, somewhat
kindly,
had on a gold wedding ring and new black
shoes. I'd probably remember him next time but
there was a good chance I
wouldn't. (with most guys if
they don't punch you in the mouth or try to
steal your woman
there isn't much to remember.)
well, Joe
I asked
how you doing?

I'm doing o.k.
he said.

how are the women treating you?
I asked.

I've got no
complaints
he said.

what are you doing for a
buck?
I asked.

oh, I got a few projects going
he said.

Joe lifted his drink and puffed on his
cigarette.

I lifted my drink and thought about
lighting a cigarette.

Benny lifted his drink
sipped
sat it down and lit a
cigarette.

well
Benny asked
how you doing?

my skin's too greasy
I have nightmares
and sometimes I think
that the substance is in the
terror.

Joe & Benny
amused
leaned forward

it was going to be a wonderful night
for me
that no Alka-Seltzer would cure for
them.

TOP GUN

just finished reading an article about myself,
quite salutary, which stated that I was
probably the most imitated writer in
America.

then I went out and got into my spa.
it was nighttime and the underwater light
shone up through the roaring jets
as the moon filtered down through the
overhanging guava tree.

well, you fat fool, I asked, have you
tricked them all, including yourself?
aren't you ashamed?

no, I replied, I did nothing
wrong.

then I shifted my bulk, reached and
hit the button, went from plain jets
to jets and bubbles.

much more
invigorating.

IT'S STRANGE

it doesn't seem so long ago that I was reading
Pound, Jeffers, Auden, Lawrence.
it doesn't seem so long ago that I was young,
living in old rooming houses.
it doesn't seem so long ago that women were
unattainable.
it doesn't seem so long ago that I had
no automobile, no telephone, no bank account.
it doesn't seem so long ago that I tried to
be a writer,
stopped for a long time and then tried once
again.

Pound, Jeffers, Auden, Lawrence don't seem
so far away or long ago.

tiny rooms and old typewriters; long
empty days; singular unforgettable
nights.

it's almost as if I could suddenly spin around now in
this room and see myself again as I was:
stubborn and starving.

it was a grand time
not so long ago.

tonight I spoke to a man on the telephone who is
coming from Germany to take photos and to interview
me
for a weekly magazine, for my
70th birthday.
and when I hung up I was sure I could hear
Pound, Jeffers, Auden, and Lawrence
laughing in the
dark.

EXPLOSION

as I angle between traffic the radio sings to me.
the Angel of Death smiles.
the sun splashes on the windshield, cleansing
the floating ghosts of my dead past.

I put it to the floor and the machine leaps
forward beautifully.
the Angel of Death continues to smile
as I hold it at an even 80.

I am between dream and reality, I am ageless.
my lost childhood reaches out a long arm and touches
me.
the dogs of my youth sit pressed eagerly side by
side on the rear seat.
my mother speaks to me again: "smile,

Henry, why are you always so sad?"
"you don't understand," I reply.

I exit the freeway and once on the boulevard
I see the burned city.
my city.
everybody's city.
city of the
world.

but I am unmoved inside my automobile
as inside my head
a gorgeous yellow flower
slowly
opens.

then I'm at the racetrack.
I am in my lane moving to the parking lot.
I park, get out, stand.
I stretch my arms 2,000 feet into
the sky.

the horses sense my arrival.
the horses acknowledge me.
they say, "we will run for you.
we love you.
we all love you."

the universe applauds as I
take one step after the
other.
one step after the other
to where
it all
begins
again.

SMALL TALK

all right, while we are gently celebrating tonight
and while crazy classical music leaps at me from
my small radio, I light a fresh cigar
and realize that I am still very much alive and that
the 21st century is almost upon me!

I walk softly now toward 5 a.m. this dark night.
my 5 cats have been in and out, looking after
me, I have petted them, spoken to them, they
are full of their own private fears wrought by previous
centuries of cruelty and abuse
but I think that they love me as much as they
can, anyhow, what I am trying to say here
is that writing is just as exciting and mad and
just as big a gamble for me as it ever was, because Death
after all these years
walks around in the room with me now and speaks softly,
asking, do you still think that you are a genuine
writer? are you pleased with what you've done?
listen, let me have one of those
cigars.

help yourself, motherfucker, I say.

Death lights up and we sit quietly for a time.
I can feel him here with me.

don't you long for the ferocity
of youth? He finally asks.

not so much, I say.

but don't you regret those things
that have been lost?

not at all, I say.

don't you miss, He asks slyly, the young girls
climbing through your window?

all they brought was bad news, I tell him

but the *illusion*, He says, don't you miss the
illusion?

hell yes, don't you? I ask.

I have no illusions, He says sadly.

sorry, I forgot about that, I say, then walk
to the window
unafraid and strangely satisfied
to watch the warm dawn
unfold.

BASIC

the short poem
like the short life
may not be the best thing
but generally
it's
easier.

this is a short
poem at the end
of a
long
life

sitting here
looking at
you
now

then
saying
adios!